Cabernet

TO

Zinfandel

FLAVORS, PAIRINGS, AND
PERSONALITIES OF THE WORLD'S MOST
POPULAR WINES

SHEA SANDERSON

To request permissions, email: contact@nouveaupress.com

ISBN: 978-1-7356753-0-5 (paperback)
ISBN : 978-1-7356753-1-2 (e-book)

First Edition: September 2020.

Edited by Nicky Guerreiro
Typesetting by Derek Murphy
Book and Cover design by Shea Sanderson

Published by Nouveau Press in the United States of America.
www.nouveaupress.com
For author info, visit www.sheasanderson.com

For my parents, who never mistook my love for wine as a drinking problem. Thank you for never staging an intervention. If you had, I would've never finished this book.

CONTENTS

INTRODUCTION

I WAS DOING JUST FINE, drinking my six-dollar bottles of Yellowtail and Barefoot. They were fast, cheap, and went down easy. That was all I really asked for from a bottle. Until one night, I got bored. Having seen everything of interest on Netflix and not really in the mood for an actual movie, I perused the documentaries.

One stood out: *Somm*. I didn't know what pulled me in, exactly. Maybe it was the movie poster. More than likely it was the strangely foreboding tagline: "The thirst for knowledge is just the beginning." I should've known then what I was about to get myself into.

After an hour and forty minutes of watching four young men strive to pass their Master Sommelier exam (which has one of the lowest pass rates in the world), I was floored. I couldn't believe what I had just seen. Suddenly, my life as an adult who regularly drank cheap wine was over. Watching these guys pick out scents like "fresh can of tennis balls", and "fresh cut garden hose" from a glass of white wine was both ridiculous and awe-inspiring. I couldn't stand the thought that I had been under-appreciating wine for the last six years. In limiting my understanding of what wine could be, what it could taste like, I was selling myself short. From that moment forward, I declared it my mission to become well-versed in wine.

There was only one problem: how does one become well-versed in wine? I figured books would help. So, I bought a couple. One on wine tasting for beginners and another on wine in general—a more comprehensive overview, if you will, of the relevant grapes, regions, science—you know, the basics. I read them both cover to cover, with a fervent desire to absorb as much information as possible. I completed a few tasting exercises from book one, bought a handful of unfamiliar wines from book two. Wash, rinse, repeat. And then one day, I hit a wall.

There was no way I would ever know as much about wine as a sommelier, and to be honest, I had no intention of becoming one. So, why was I trying to learn all of this useless information? Why did I feel the need to know all there was to know about wine? So I could appear more cultured? More sophisticated? So I had some idea of what to do when I encountered a wine list at a restaurant? No, maybe, and dear God, yes. But I realized that the way I had gone about my wine education was all wrong. I didn't care about fermentation. I didn't care about Brettanomyces. I didn't even care about the differences between American and French oak. In fact, I didn't need most of the information I was reading. All I cared about was what certain wines tasted like. And maybe knowing when to choose one wine over another for a dinner party, a cookout, a holiday, a happy hour—whatever. That was it, the sum total of my wine desires. But for whatever reason, finding this simple information was more difficult than it looked.

A lot of available books on wine seemed to fall into two categories: how to drink wine (as if we need instructions) and wine encyclopedia, neither of which were really what I needed. Halfway through learning how to drink wine, I realized that most of the information was useless. Learning how to swirl, sniff, slosh, spit, is not a top priority when you really just want to drink it like a normal human being. Knowing what makes a wine organic or not would not help me pick out a bottle of red to bring to my friend's dinner. Again, no one was telling me how to confidently choose wines. They just tried to tell me how to drink it like a "professional". Since I didn't care about looking like a sommelier, those books were out.

The other category, wine encyclopedia, just inundates you with endless information on wine regions, wine-making, growing conditions, terroir, blah, blah, blah. I didn't need to know everything there is to know about Bordeaux, France and how long wine has been growing there, no offense to the Bordelais. What I wanted to know was what a Bordeaux tasted like, or when and where to drink it. So, as quickly as it had come, my newfound fascination with wine stopped. No one was providing the information I actually needed, so why bother? My frustration drove me away from trying to learn about wine for months. It wasn't until about a year ago when it finally hit me: if I ever wanted to learn how to choose wines confidently, I was going to have to rethink my approach.

I had already invested too much time and energy to give up on wine altogether. I didn't want to be a wine expert. I just wanted to conquer the wine aisle at a liquor store, the wine list at a restaurant. So I set out on my own, a wine renegade fielding the endless aisles at Binny's with only one goal: choose one and see what it tastes like. That was it. That was how I would learn about wine. If I wanted to talk about Cabernet Sauvignon with any sort of confidence, I needed to try Cabernet Sauvignon. Not only try, but spend time with it. Taste it intentionally. Pay attention to the flavors. Heck, learn about flavors by tasting a bunch of them. And then decide: like or dislike? Why or why not? It was simple. It was replicable. And I could do it with any wine, from any region, and within my budget. All I needed to do was make a plan. So, I started with the most popular wine varieties in the world. 25, to be exact. And now, here I am, about to share what I've learned with you.

I've always been of the belief that if you can't find what you're looking for, create it yourself. That's what this book is; the overview of wine that I wish I'd had when I first started. It's both a collection of profiles of the world's most popular wines and grapes and a guide to learning about them the same way I had. It's for me as much as it is for you. And, as you continue on, you'll see I intended it that way.

Within these pages, you'll find 25 individual wine and grape profiles—16 red, 9 white. Each one is based on the information I found most helpful for understanding each wine's unique characteristics, in the hopes you find it helpful, too. You'll find that each wine or grape starts with an introduction— what wines the grape makes, regional name variations, if any, where it's grown, and its reputation within the wine world (and in my opinion).

Following the introduction, I include tasting notes from an exemplary bottle of my choosing. I chose the bottles based on price (most under $20), region (one of the top three that grow the grape), and availability (I found 90% were at Binny's, a wine superstore, and the remaining 10% from my local liquor store). Some bottles in the book were rated highly by critics; some weren't rated at all. I didn't care about a critic's taste more than my own, so I didn't prioritize their ratings.

Keep in mind, my tasting notes are by no means comprehensive. I still can't taste mocha or bramble (?) in a glass of red wine, even though a lot of wine critics can. I simply share what I taste in a particular wine, in as straight-forward a way as I knew how. I share what the wine feels like when you drink it, what flavors I smell and taste, and any clarifying descriptions of its acidity and tannins (the two most important 'structural' descriptors of wine).

Finally, wrapping up each grape's profile, there's the "In the Wild" section. This section serves one of two purposes: to assign the wine a personality, or to give it context within your life. Some wines have personalities I liken to generic characters, like an Italian uncle or a well-traveled aunt. Others have specific personality traits that embody what the wine is all about. That's one way in which "In the Wild" is used.

The other is to give the wine context within a person's life. We can look up food and wine pairings easily these days. But life and wine pairings, not so much. Some wines in this book pair well with certain circumstances and scenarios in life, like meeting your significant other's parents, having an existential crisis, or a Friday night in watching Annie Hall for the 47th time. My goal is to help each wine variety become memorable based on more than just its flavors. Besides, remembering flavor profiles is way too hard, especially since a lot of wines have similar tasting notes. But remembering which wine goes well with a business dinner with your boss or which wine reminds you of tea with Grandma is much easier.

You'll notice that some wine profiles will have a snippet on finding a French bottle, prior to the introduction. In France, it's much more common to list the region that the wine was grown in (i.e. Meursault) on the label instead of the varietal (i.e. Chardonnay). That means that if you don't know where the French grow Chardonnay, you'll have to look up every label on your phone wasting time that could be spent drinking. Keep in mind that France doesn't grow every wine variety in this book, so not all wine profiles will have a snippet. But for those grapes that it does grow, I've listed the regions and their most common appellations to guide your search.

After trial and error, this is how I've learned to make sense of wine. The pertinent (and brief) background information, the tasting, and the context of the wine itself. By no means is my profiling meant to be gospel on these iconic grapes. I'm not a wine-maker, a wine critic, or even a credentialed anybody in the world of wine. But I saw a problem that needed a solution, and I set out to make sense of wine for my sake. Now, it's my hope that this book can serve as a solution for others who are stuck like I once was.

Wine doesn't have to be hard to learn about. It doesn't require pomp and circumstance or a sommelier's certification to be understood and enjoyed. It just needs people who are willing to spend time with it. Savoring it, learning from it, and including it in everyday life. If that's the kind of wine relationship you're after, then I hope you come out of this ready to enjoy wine as it was intended. If you don't, that's okay. No one should police how or why you drink wine. But if you decide that at the end of this book, you're ready to start a tasting journey of your own, hoping to learn like I have, just remember…

"The thirst for knowledge is just the beginning."

WHITE WINES & GRAPES

"Always keep a bottle of Champagne in the fridge for special occasions. Sometimes, the special occasion is that you've got a bottle of Champagne in the fridge." – *Hester Browne, author*

CAVA

IT'S SHOCKING EVERY TIME I encounter someone who doesn't enjoy sparkling wine. And it's always for the same reason: "I don't like the bubbles." Yet, I can find those same people drinking vodka sodas or just plain Sprite without blinking an eye. So what is it, then? Is it the fault of the commonly purchased "brut" variety, which isn't a sweet adventure? Is it the cost demanded by a bottle of Veuve? What is it, sparkler haters?! If it's the "brut," opt for a "sec"—it's sweeter for your sensitive palate. If it's the price of Champagne, then that's valid—but you should look at other sparkling wines that are equal in taste and quality, and which cost much less. Enter Cava, the Spanish sparkler.

The process of making Cava is nearly identical to that of Champagne, so you know the quality is there from the start. But I guess Spain just wants the world to drink their sparkling wine more than France does, and chooses to undercut Champagne by selling Cava at half the price. If there's one way to convince people to drink your bubbles, it's making it just as well as your competitors and selling it at a bargain. If you're not convinced by now, I don't know what to tell you. Spain knows what it's doing when it comes to wine. Whether it's red, white, or sparkling, you can't miss out on the quality of wines that Spain is producing, especially considering how wallet-friendly they are. Cava is a prime example.

THE TASTING

THE BOTTLE: *Flama d'Or Semi-Sec. Catalonia, Spain. $10.*

With sparkling wine, it's always fun to experiment, especially if the price is right. Having always enjoyed "brut" sparkling wines, I thought I might give "semi-sec," a sweeter variety, a try. By way of reference, sparkling wines range in sweetness, from Brut Nature (the driest variety) to Dulce (the sweetest). In between, you'll find:

Brut Nature (driest) > Extra Brut > Brut > Extra Seco > Seco > Semi-Seco > Dulce (sweetest)

Having had no frame of reference for what any Cava tastes like, regardless of its sweetness, this bottle tasting was as blind and fresh as you can get. In the glass, its color was unlike any Champagne or Prosecco I've ever had. It's the exact color of straw; not the dried kind—the greenish-yellow, fresh, wet straw color. And it smells like halved green grapes and honey.

The taste is perfect. Just like the sparkling white grape juice you used to have during the holidays when you were nine, but with a bit of honey and green apple added. The bubbles are effervescent, lingering on just the tip of your tongue and balancing out the sweetness nicely.

Despite being a habitual "brut" drinker, venturing out into the sweeter "semi-seco" territory was not nearly as saccharine as I expected. It's a sweet deviation that doesn't leave you with a raging hangover the next day (trust me, I drank the entire bottle and lived to see another day). Tasting across the sweetness spectrum isn't so bad after all.

IN THE WILD

It's the ideal summer day. Hot, but not humid. It's sunny, but not without an ever-present breeze. You're spending the day by the pool, slathered in coconut-scented sunscreen, the sounds of the water lapping in front of you soothing you into bliss. You're enveloped in warmth but not sweltering. The wafts of chlorine remind you of the nearby oasis. You wish every day were like this. To further enhance a near perfect day, you retrieve a bottle of semi-seco Cava that's been waiting patiently in the refrigerator, chilling. A sparkler waiting for its match.

Once poured into glasses not normally suited for poolside, it comes to life. The elegance of the glass flutes, the lightest shade of fresh straw, glistening with a delicate smattering of bubbles. It's a sublime stamp marking the glorious days of summer, with the cooling green grape and apple flavors coated in a light drizzle of honey. You've captured sun-kissed sweetness in your glass, and it's everything you never knew you needed. The heavenly day finally marked with perfection, all thanks to a semi-seco bottle of Cava.

CHAMPAGNE

Note: Champagne only comes from Champagne, France.
Every other wine with bubbles is simply sparkling wine.

WHAT'S LEFT TO SAY ABOUT Champagne that hasn't already been said? It's the toast of the town, the essence of Jay Gatsby, the New Year's Eve elixir poured ceremoniously at the stroke of midnight. Champagne is iconic, in a league of its own. It will never die, as long as France still has grapes to grow and willing vintners to tend to them. And while it's easy to fall into the trap of assuming all champagnes taste the same, allow me a simple rebuttal: the bubbles may be identical, but the underlying flavors have more to say.

Once upon a time, and maybe even still, it was thought that the more money you spent on a bottle of Champagne, the better it would taste. Having tasted $5 bottles and a $250 bottle (and at every price point in between), I think that's a bunch of bull. But I will say that, flavor-wise, there's a world of difference. On the low end, you get what you pay for—bubbles, acidity, and not much else. On the high end, you get a lot of toasty flavor. Somewhere in the middle, at around $40, is where the flavors really start to bloom.

THE TASTING

THE BOTTLE: *Moët & Chandon Impérial Brut NV. Champagne, France. $40.*

In the spirit of full disclosure, I did not spend $40 on this bottle, because I did not buy a full bottle. I just needed enough to thoroughly taste with, two glasses worth to be exact, and a 187 mL bottle fits that bill perfectly at just $13. Feel free to take that trick home with you when you do at-home tastings of your own, *wink wink*.

When buying or ordering Champagne, you usually have two options: Veuve Clicquot or Moët & Chandon. Unless you're trying to waste your money to exude high-roller status, in which case you're buying Dom Perignon. But no one needs to do that anymore. Your taste in Champagne will not impress people as much as you think it will—it just makes them want to put their drinks on your tab every chance they get. So, again, two options. Having had Veuve before on birthdays and New

Year's celebrations, it was time to dabble with Mr. Moët for a change.

On the surface, it's a dead ringer for Veuve. A trained eye couldn't tell the difference. In the glass, it's pale yellow with a lively smattering of bubbles. However, the smell is distinct from Veuve's toast and citrus notes. Instead, Moët delights with aromas of fresh brioche bread and a hint of pear. The two champagne powerhouses are already starting to pull apart in their flavors.

The first taste cements it. The flavors are of perfectly ripe Anjou pear, with a drop of cassis liqueur, on top of toasted brioche. It's bright, the tiniest bit sweet (it is a "brut," after all), and the acidity stays just on the tip of your tongue while the rest of your mouth coats with the pear and brioche flavor. If you wait long enough for a second sip, it finishes smoothly with an almost pastry cream-like essence.

Having spent quality time with both Veuve and now Moët, the flavors are worlds apart. While the Veuve has more ginger and toasted almond flavors to hold your mouth captive, the Moët is more pastry-sweet in flavor, and opens up the door for another sip as soon as you're ready.

IN THE WILD

Champagne is known far and wide as the centerpiece of celebrations. Making the right choice of Champagne is of the utmost importance. For the overzealous, punchy-with-excitement sort of celebration, Veuve is your party girl. Maybe you landed a promotion, maybe you're embarking on the most obnoxious bachelorette party of your entire life, maybe it's a 21st birthday—whatever the brand of loud you're going for, Veuve has the flavor to match.

For those celebrations full of reverence and sentimentality, Moët should be there. Whether it's an adult (refined, not X-rated) birthday, a going-away or long-awaited housewarming party, Moët's pastry-essence will tie together a time-honored or sentimental occasion. But either way you go, Champagne won't disappoint. It's impossible to even *say* "bubbles" and be mad, let alone to drink them. So celebrate often and make sure the wine's sparkling. Because life without effervescence is a flat life not worth living.

CHARDONNAY

To find a French bottle, look in: Chablis, Burgundy (Bourgogne Blanc), and Burgundy's villages Côte de Beaune (Meursault, Montrachet, Corton, Saint-Aubin), Mâcon, Pouilly-Fuissé, and Côte Chalonnaise (Rully, Montagny)

WHEN I SAY CHARDONNAY, YOU say... suburban moms named Karen, right? I can't blame you. Whoever is in charge of PR for oaky Chardonnay has really done no favors for this delicious little grape. More often than not, its reputation is cliched and banal instead of sophisticated and revered. It's a shame, really, that people dismiss and look down on it simply because of its unfairly perpetuated rep—especially in California (don't shoot the messenger, Californians—I don't agree!). To the haters who pooh-pooh Kendall-Jackson like you're trying for gold stars in snobbery: what did an oaked Chardonnay ever do to you, huh?!

I'll tell you what it did. It cemented itself as one of the most popular wine grapes in the world. It's so popular that it has fancy-sounding, wildly different alter egos in France: Chablis and Bourgogne Blanc, for example. And guess what? Champagne is almost always made with Chardonnay grapes. So, don't tell me it's for tasteless amateurs. Your fancy bottle of Dom is half Chardonnay, buddy. Now let's give it the respect it deserves, shall we? Oaked or unoaked, Californian or French, Chardonnay can delight. You just have to decide where to get a glass.

THE TASTING

THE BOTTLE: *Kendall-Jackson Vintner's Reserve Chardonnay 2018. Santa Rosa, CA. $13.*

Oaked Chardonnays are very distinct: creamy in texture and bursting with flavors of butter, baking spices, vanilla, or even caramel. Their unoaked counterparts are notably different: light and crisp, with non-tropical fruit and citrus.

The presence of oak in a wine is polarizing—some prefer it, some can't stand it. Chardonnay is notably a wine where you'll have to pick a side. For "Team Oak," picking a Chardonnay from California or Australia will more often than not give you the oaky flavor you crave. For "Team No-Oak," French varieties, such as Chablis, will give you more crisp, mineral flavors.

Today, we taste the queen of oaked California Chardonnay: Kendall-Jackson. Known for its quintessential buttery flavors, you can't know oaky Chardonnay until you've danced with its heaviest hitter. And Kendall-Jackson's wines reign supreme.

On the nose, there's pear, pineapple, and a hint of white flowers—perhaps magnolia or even gardenia. Lovely. But you can't expect anything less from a queen, can you?

The flavors are a perfect blend of buttered toast, white peach, and ripe pineapple. The pineapple is so ripe it's bordering on tart, similar to when you eat too much pineapple in one sitting and your mouth starts to pucker. That tart fruit flavor mixed with buttered toast is what the 2018 is all about. It's tropical, smooth, and just the slightest bit buttery, although not nearly as buttery as years prior.

The fruit flavors are very concentrated, allowing the buttery taste to come through as a secondary flavor. This is odd for K-J, seeing as how "buttered popcorn" is usually one of the first flavors you get with their Chardonnays. A prime example that even when you stick with the same winemaker year after year, vintages can differ in flavor thanks to the wildly unpredictable effect of weather and growing conditions.

IN THE WILD

Seeing as how Chardonnay is one of the two reasons that California deserves respect in the wine world (the other being Cabernet Sauvignon), it would make sense that any Cali-adjacent situation would warrant a glass. Let's say, for example, a crisp 60° summer evening, the breeze cool but not quite chilly. You're wearing your go-to North Face or Patagonia zip up and your most lived-in pair of Levi's while the theme song from *Big Little Lies* plays on repeat in the background (in your mind or out loud—Chardonnay isn't picky).

The vibe is relaxed, yet composed. Lovely, yet still approachable. It's the atmosphere Chardonnay was made for. And if you find yourself inspired to re-watch *Big Little Lies*, make sure you take a rich, buttery piece of California along for the ride.

CHENIN BLANC

To find a French bottle, look in: the Loire (Vouvray, Savannières)

KNOWN AS VOUVRAY IN FRANCE and Steen in South Africa, Chenin Blanc is as dynamic a grape as they come. It can produce sparkling wines made in the same traditional method made famous by Champagne. It can bring forth light and crisp wines for those who normally drink dry Rieslings or Sauvignon Blancs. It can even transform into a rich aromatic version of itself, not unlike an oaked Chardonnay. Never mind the fact that it's capable of producing sweet dessert wines, too. Like I said, as dynamic as they come.

Is Chenin Blanc deeply underrated? Yes. Is it able to transform to match the tastes of any white wine drinker?

Yes. Are there myriad regions around the world that make Chenin well? Yes. Are you still unconvinced that Chenin is worth a tasting excursion? Better not be. For any avid white wine drinker (or any wine drinker in general), Chenin Blanc is worthy of much more attention than is currently being paid. In fact, the chances of you regretting the choice to deviate from your regularly scheduled white wines in favor of a Chenin are about as high as finding a white giraffe in Africa. Not likely.

THE TASTING

THE BOTTLE: *MAN Family Wines Chenin Blanc 2016. Paarl, South Africa. $9.*

South Africa is famous for its lovely, oil-slicked, aromatic Chenin Blancs—historically known as Steen in the local parlance. And at the MAN winery, free-run Steen is one step above. They make their wines solely from "free-run juice," that is, juice that's naturally released from the grapes as their skins split under their own weight, without being mechanically pressed. In France, this free-run juice is known as "vin de goutte" or "noble juice," deemed the highest-quality and the purest expression of flavor from the grape itself.

What can one expect from this free-run South African Chenin Blanc? First, a deep golden color akin to a California Chardonnay. Mingling aromas of pineapple, guava, and pear offer another layer. But the taste... the taste is where the free-run really stands out.

Baked yellow apple, ripe white peach, and oily Meyer lemon all dance together. Unlike any other white wine with acidity, this free-run variety stands still in your mouth. The slight oily texture and beautifully balanced flavors suspend themselves in your mouth, should you hold it in and savor your sip. The acidity doesn't eventually wear down your tongue like most dry white wines do. It's an acidic acrobatic feat attributed to the pure expression of the free-run juice.

South Africa makes 50% of the world's Chenin Blanc for a reason. It's vibrant, golden, and slick enough to make you truly want to slow down and enjoy the pristine Steen. And for just $9, sampling this free-run production is more than worth it every time.

IN THE WILD

Summer needs Steen, and you'll be dying without it. Chardonnay is just the slightest bit too rich. Pinot Grigio is too thin. And Sauvignon Blanc tastes too much like a jungle to be any reprieve from a grossly humid summer day.

When it's tropically hot out, a chilled glass of South African Chenin Blanc is the perfect elixir to cut through the thick, stifling heat. It's an oasis bursting with ripe yellow fruits, invigorating kisses of acidity, and an oily slick texture that completely coats your mouth with the remnant chill still dripping off the bottle. It's refreshing—a liquid life jacket rescuing you from the suffocating humidity.

Summer. South Africa. Free-run Steen. What more can you ask for?

MUSCAT BLANC

To find a French bottle, look in: Alsace; unlike the rest of France, they label according to grape varieties

UNBEKNOWNST TO ME, MUSCAT BLANC and I have a lengthy history. One of the first wines I ever had more than an unwilling sip of, it ushered me in to the world of wine with its sweetness and feminine reputation. Now, eight years later, I've realized that Muscat Blanc is the grape responsible for the raucous wine nights of girls in college: in the guise of the infamous Moscato.

You'd think the grape's name would lend itself to a higher class of drinking—pinkies out, airs put on. But if you mash it up, put it in a $5 bottle of Barefoot, and call it Moscato, you've got yourself a drunken Tuesday night in college where hordes of women come together, one bottle deep each, and boldly call it "wine night." Those nights, compounded week after week in college, are the reason so many of us never again return to Moscato after we graduate. So you could say I feel like I'm returning to a former life that I've outgrown, sitting across from an exorbitantly priced (compared to my college budget) bottle of Moscato.

The only intrigue here is that I'm not returning to the scene of the crime: the $5 value section of bargain bin wine. If I'm to give Muscat Blanc its fair shake, I have to clear the $15 price mark to find quality. So, I guess the real question is: Muscat Blanc—overlooked or overdone? Let's find out.

THE TASTING

THE BOTTLE: *Michele Chiarlo Nivole Moscato d'Asti 2018. Piedmont, Italy. $17.*

Prior to having an Italian Barbera from Asti, I had always assumed that "d'Asti" signified a wine that was gently fizzy. Moscato d'Astis are always a little bubbly, while plain Moscato is not. So, when the Barbera I tried ended up not sparkling, I was confused. My deductive reasoning was sound, but wrong. While Asti is a region in Italy *known for* its sweet sparkling wines, the fizz doesn't necessarily apply to the red wines of the region. Lesson learned. White wine d'Astis = fizzy. Red wine d'Astis = not so much.

But seeing as how this bottle of Michele Chiarlo doesn't have a cork, I was expecting a still variety of Moscato. You can't have bubbles without a cork present, right? Wrong. Upon first pour, a thin layer of fizz rose to the top of the glass. I guess you don't need a cork to experience bubbles after all.

Fizzy surprise aside, this Moscato is a lovely pale straw color and smells distinctly and sweetly floral, almost perfume-like. Maybe gardenias? Or maybe orange blossoms? It's the white-flower perfume that graces the napes of Estée Lauder-loving moms, aunts, or grandmas. The resemblance is chilling.

The flavors are thankfully distinct from the $5 Barefoot bottles of my collegiate days. It's organic honey—the kind that comes in a jar, mostly solidified and crystallized—with apricot, canned mandarin oranges in syrup, and floral perfume. It's fragrant and fruit-syrupy sweet accompanied by a gentle, bubbling fizz. It's considerably more aromatic and floral than any $5 bottle you'll find.

Sampling above the $15 price range, Muscat Blanc from Asti offers a truly aromatic white wine laced with a feminine fizz and syrupy sweetness. An elevated version, yes, but still a sweet white wine to the core.

IN THE WILD

Moscato d'Asti is the quintessential wine to have when meeting Grandma for tea, brunch, or any time before she falls asleep at 8 p.m. It smells just like her, with overpowering floral perfume. It matches her barrage of complimentary sweetness with its syrupy fruit flavors. Plus, Moscato is notoriously low in alcohol, so you don't have to worry about accidentally getting sloshed with Nana (unless that's her preference—grandmas have earned the right to do whatever they want).

What once was for drunken Tuesday nights in college has turned into the centerpiece of afternoons with Grandma. But only if you fork over some extra cash. But honestly, isn't Grandma worth it?

PINOT GRIS

To find a French bottle, look in: Alsace; unlike the rest of France, they label according to grape varieties

PINOT GRIS AND PINOT GRIGIO: they're made from the same grape, but different in flavor. Often interchangeable, but not identical. Is it confusing? For sure. Luckily, it's easy to understand the Pinot Gris/Grigio distinction. Pinot Gris is the grape used in both Pinot Gris (naturally) and Pinot Grigio wines. Why the wines are named differently when they come from the same grape has everything to do with what style they're made in—Italian-style Grigio or Alsatian-style Gris.

In Italy, and any other region in the world choosing to adopt the Italian style, Pinot Grigio is much more crisp, dry, and laced with minerality (think of the smell and taste of wet rocks).

Conversely, in the French style, Pinot Gris has more ripe fruit flavor and Meyer lemon citrus notes. Easy peasy, Pinot Grig-y. Although, if you get a Pinot Gris from Alsace, specifically, you'll end up with a sweeter version of Pinot Gris than you'd find in Oregon, for example.

Either way you go, Gris or Grigio, you'll get an elegant white wine that's full of acidity to perk you right out of your summer slumber. It's clean, it's lucid, and it's well-balanced, making it perfect for drinking alone or with a lighter-bodied meal. Whether you err on the side of fruitier flavors in your white wines or lean towards the dry, minerally end of the spectrum, the Pinot Gris grape can morph to fit your tastes. You need only pick a style.

THE TASTING

THE BOTTLE: *Portlandia Pinot Gris 2019. Willamette, Oregon. $15.*

Pinot Gris from Oregon, not Alsace, will generally be fruitier in flavor. This one is no different, as evidenced by the wafts of green apple, citrus, and honeysuckle aroma. If you're not sure what honeysuckle smells like, it's a fruity and warm-scented flower that smells like honey and ripe citrus. Exactly the scent of this wine in the glass. Ever the elegant white, the color is such a light shade of straw yellow it's almost crystalline. Give it a swirl in your glass, and you'll know exactly what I mean.

The tasting experience is no less lovely. Pear, green apple skin, Meyer lemon, and the slightest bit of wet gravel coat the entirety of your mouth. From the tip of your tongue to the inside crevices of your cheeks, the acidity livens things right up, while the fruit, citrus, and mineral flavors take their time on your tongue. To say Pinot Gris is a refreshing grape would be the understatement of the century. It's bright, lucid, and invigorating, with just enough fruit to keep it poised. Add a chill to it, and it's the ideal antidote for a summer day, heavy with dry heat. Perfection.

IN THE WILD

Pinot Gris is exquisite, the ideal guest at a dinner enjoyed outside on a restaurant patio during August or still-warm September, twinkle lights strung up on trees between cozy tables. For dinner, a nicely paired roasted chicken, or maybe you're indulging in the last scallops of the season before October arrives. The breeze is cool and intermittent, the days slowly getting shorter. Indian summer is creeping in, and Pinot Gris is its prelude.

It's refined, crisp, and lovely—the wine that transforms its drinker into the picture of sophistication and elegance. When drinking it, you know exactly who you are, what you think, and seem to hold a timeless mastery over life. All of this is to be had from an abiding gray grape grown in the midst of rich volcanic soil. Quite the transformation, indeed.

PROSECCO

FINE, I'LL SAY IT: CHAMPAGNE does not belong at breakfast. The sooner we all realize that, the more money we can all save at our next bottomless brunch. Sure, Andre is $5, but is it doing your mimosa bar any favors? Prosecco exists for a reason. I know it's easy to lump all the sparkling wines together, but in fact, Prosecco stands on its own.

Where Champagne is marketed as a luxury and is bottled with 5-7 atmospheres of pressure, producing longer-lasting bubbles, Prosecco is affordable and maintains 2-4 atmospheres for a gentle, fleeting fizz. Where Cava is made in a process very similar to Champagne and maintains its high acidity, Prosecco is made in a less time-intensive way and yields much fruitier flavors. To compare the three would be like comparing apples to raspberries to oranges. Some major things in common, yes, but there are far more significant differences to discuss. Where Prosecco shines apart from the others is its ability to complement a wide variety of dishes, making it the ideal sipper for any occasion.

The fruitiness of Prosecco makes a mimosa of any flavor brighter without overpowering it. The soft sweetness can temper a spicy Asian dish or liven up a mild-flavored one. And the gentle bubbles make for a perfect apéritif any time of day. Prosecco shines where Cava and Champagne can't. And an extra-dry variety is the perfect example of that.

THE TASTING

THE BOTTLE: *Ruffino Prosecco NV. Veneto, Italy. $13.*

Ruffino is an extra-dry Prosecco, a perfect harmony of acid and sweet that is worth exploring even if you always err on the "brut" side of things. Extra-dry is the perfect middle ground between the bone-dry and acidic "brut" and the tad-too-sweet "dry" variety, although fans of either could easily enjoy the Ruffino without feeling slighted.

The distinctive fruitiness of Prosecco is apparent as soon as you smell it. Green apple, citrus, and sourdough bread aromas all come through gently, the bubbles small enough to not pop on the surface (and, consequently, in your nose).

The taste is a similar experience. Just-ripe golden apples, a slice of nectarine, and with a finish of sweet cream, the Ruffino is delicately balanced. Where the "brut" would be much more acidic and feel far more bubbly, the acid in the extra-dry is cut cleanly with a fruity, smooth, and creamy finish—the bubbles appearing and flickering as you taste.

Trust me—the "extra-dry" style of Prosecco is worth a departure from your norm. It's infallible.

IN THE WILD

It's brunch. You're outside in a garden, or maybe just a restaurant patio with enough lush landscaping to feel like a garden. It's the first warm day of spring, and people are starting to dress out of the winter comfort zone of blacks, navys, and grays. For the first time all year, there's color all around—pinks, oranges, yellows. The requisite dark sunglasses, both a chic accessory and a shield to hide the number of morning drinks already consumed, are poised.

A bottle of 'extra-dry' Prosecco is chilling in an aluminum bucket in the middle of your table, waiting patiently for the next flute to run dry. The minute one does, it's ready to flood into the glass, preparing to intertwine with whatever juice was selected for the morning. Without the Prosecco, the juice is just sugar with pockets of tartness. But with it, it's vibrant. It's effervescent, fruitier, rippling with flavors you can't get from a single source. And as quickly as it appeared, bursting with flavor, it leaves with nothing left behind but a kiss of vanilla cream.

Prosecco is what other sparkling wines could never be: affable, harmonizing, and delicate. And, of course, the rightful guardian of brunch.

RIESLING

To find a French bottle, look in: Alsace; unlike the rest of France, they label according to grape varieties

IT'S HARD NOT TO FEEL bad for Riesling. So many people assume that all Rieslings are sweet and, therefore, not worth their time. After all, any serious wine drinker would *never* touch a white wine that wasn't bone-dry (said no one ever). It's true that most Rieslings have a hint of residual sugar to balance out their high acidity. But not all Rieslings temper their tartness. Case in point, Alsace in France, Austria, Washington, and New York all produce dry Rieslings. You can also find bottles of "Trocken," Germany's dry variety.

So, one could say that writing off Riesling for being sweet is an oversight on any drinker's part. Take a quick look around, and you'll easily find a lean, dry version to suit your tastes. Although, the aromatics alone are worth incorporating a Riesling into your repertoire from time to time, even if it isn't a bone-dry variety. Whether as a standalone sipper or a spicy cuisine counterpart, Riesling can fit into a surprising number of drinkable pockets. You just have to put your limited preconceptions to the side to realize it.

THE TASTING

THE BOTTLE: *August Kesseler R Riesling Kabinett 2018. Rheingau, Germany. $13.*

Not being one to shy away from an off-dry white wine (meaning, not bone-dry, but slightly sweeter), I find that a Riesling of any variety is always welcome. The 'Kabinett' designation on this bottle signifies a potentially dry to off-dry wine—either way, you're in good shape as long as you're not averse to residual sugar. If you're unsure, a simple smell can often tell you how dry the wine will end up being.

The August Kesseler smells off-dry, like ripe honey crisp apple, Meyer lemon, and sharp, sweet jasmine. In the glass, it's very pale yellow in color, light and easily swirled, and aromatic, as almost all Rieslings are.

The taste is predictable, with notes of honey crisp apple, mandarin orange, glazed lemon cake, and, in pure Riesling fashion, hints of plastic kiddie pool—the inflatable kind, fresh out of the packaging. Some people call that smell or taste "petrol" or "petroleum wax," but kiddie pool rings truer to me. It's a flavor distinctive of Rieslings. And it's most pungent in wines from cooler climates—Washington, especially.

Upon first tasting, the overly tart green apple-like acidity bursts forward, but immediately gets tempered by the residual sugar. Good thing, too, for if it weren't for the slight sweetness, the acidity would've been too much. And this is why off-dry exists, to suspend the acid with the sweet. It's why a mandarin orange is so balanced, why a bottle of semi-seco Cava can be a delight: the balance of the two elements. And an off-dry Riesling does it well.

IN THE WILD

Is there a wine that can stand up to the red-hot flavors of spicy Asian cuisine? Allow me to introduce to you an unlikely match: the off-dry Riesling. A complementary reliever in the blazing world of Szechuan.

Tonight: your favorite Szechuan restaurant. Your order: a gluttonous sampling of various soups, noodles, and beef. All saucy, all radiating peppery heat. The Szechuan peppercorns, the hot red chilis all ignite your mouth with an effusive power. Water won't reduce it, and beer will only egg it on. You turn to a German 'Kabinett' Riesling. Its sweetness immediately tempers the flames. The pungent, floral, fruity flavors of the sweet wine don't fight with the savory flavors on the table. There's a balance here: sweet and spicy; fruity and savory. Two wildly different corners of the world bringing forth distinct flavors, both of which are seemingly made for each other. Heat and sweet proving once again that opposites attract.

SAUVIGNON BLANC

To find a French bottle, look in: the Loire (Sancerre, Pouilly-Fumé, Menetou-Salon, Reuilly, Quincy), and Bordeaux (Bordeaux Blanc, Entre-Deux-Mers, Graves)

I'LL BE HONEST, SAUVIGNON BLANC is not a grape that's easy to be impartial about. You either insist on championing the grape until your last breath, or you abhor it with the passion of a toddler refusing to eat their vegetables (an appropriate reaction, considering Sauv Blanc regularly tastes like green bell peppers). It's hard to straddle the fence on this herbaceous grape. Eventually, you'll choose a side and you'll insist that your taste is the correct one. It's almost political, now that I think about it.

Why the discord? Well, Sauvignon Blanc is distinct—almost avant-garde in its flavors. Some find its grassy, herbaceous notes refreshing, unlike any other white wine. Others find them repugnant. It evokes a knee-jerk reaction: do you want your white wine to taste primarily like lemongrass? Because no matter where in the world the Sauv Blanc you're drinking is from, it will always have *some* grassy flavor, whether it's the lead actor or a supporting role.

If you savor the grassiness, you'll love bottles from France. On the other hand, New Zealand's warmer climate yields a more subtle grassy taste that's balanced with passionfruit and tropical flavors. Either way, there's an adventure that awaits those who settle into a Sauvignon Blanc—the regional differences in flavor are enough to keep you on your toes from one bottle to the next. However, if you find you just can't get on board with lemongrass in your wine, you're not the only one.

THE TASTING

THE BOTTLE: *Fire Road Sauvignon Blanc 2018. Marlborough, New Zealand. $12.*

I fall squarely in the camp of "no, thank you" when it comes to Sauvignon Blanc. But, once upon a time, I was coerced into trying a bottle from New Zealand. The sommelier promised me it would be different—fruitier and less… offensive. The bottle: Astrolabe Sauvignon Blanc 2017. More passionfruit flavor than anything, and the grassy flavors were as subtle as I could hope for. The saving grace of Sauvignon.

Remembering this myth-busting experience, I figured I'd dip my toes back in where it's safe: Marlborough, New Zealand, the land of passionfruit-y Sauv Blanc. The Fire Road label assured it. Yes, there would be herby flavors, but passionfruit would be there to hold my hand, too. Upon pouring my first glass, I realized someone was lying.

The instant aroma was of a lawn bag full of mown grass clippings that have been sitting in the sun. Alongside it were lemon juice and the tiniest bit of white peach. The smell is classic, herbal, grassy Sauvignon Blanc. And the taste was right on par.

Fire Road tastes exactly like a soggy spinach salad with way too much lemon vinaigrette, a bit of grapefruit, and maybe three drops of passionfruit juice. It's pungent, it's citrusy, and remarkably like mown grass. And the taste lingers for quite some time. Although, the salad-like flavors do eventually subside to make more room for the secondary tropical flavors. Or maybe you just go tongue-blind, who's to say?

Either way, classicists who love the biting herb and citrus combo that Sauvignon Blanc is notorious for can still very much enjoy a fruitier variety from warmer climates like New Zealand without missing out. The notorious lemongrass flavor will never be absent, no matter where you drink from. Whether that's good news or bad, that's up to you. As for me, I'll be staying away from this darling grape for a while. At least until I can find another Astrolabe.

IN THE WILD

Pardon my French, but Sauvignon Blanc is one messy bitch. How else would there be such a divide amongst wine drinkers over one little green grape? She's determined to take over the world and doesn't care if she leaves a heated blaze of argument in her wake. She doesn't mess around, either. You can't fight her; she'll win every single time. There's no way to temper her. Even if you think you have, give it time. Her distinct flavors will come out swinging eventually. And that's just the beginning.

Sauvignon Blanc grows like an interminable weed. It literally takes over. And no matter where you are in the world, you can't manipulate it, hoping to pull the vegetal flavor out of it. It's insistent. Refusing to morph into an unrecognizable derivative, Sauvignon Blanc won't be goaded into being fruity, or more minerally. It's lean, biting, and excavating in its lemongrass flavor. It doesn't care if it's too pungent, too vegetal, too crisp. In fact, I think Sauvignon Blanc prefers the heated dispute that surrounds its flavors. A messy, distinctive, rebellious little grape. And as long as it remains polarizing and continues to bear roots in France, Sauv Blanc won't be going anywhere, anytime soon.

RED WINES & GRAPES

"It's a naïve domestic Burgundy without any breeding, but I think you'll be amused by its presumption." – James Thurber, author & cartoonist

BARBERA

IT'S TIME FOR THIS LITTLE-KNOWN grape from Italy to get its due. Pronounced like "bar-bear-uh," not à la Streisand, this grape has flown under the radar outside of its home in Italy for a while now. The treasure of Italy's northern region has always been the revered Nebbiolo grape, and its worldwide appeal has left little room for Barbera to shine. But it's not all doom and gloom for this underdog grape. More and more, people are branching out in their wine choices. As a result, they're discovering the "wines of the people" from countries around the world—Barbera included.

Good thing, because Barbera is quite the unexpected treat. Its inky color belies a surprisingly light, drinkable weight, which makes for a unique tasting experience. In fact, should you stumble upon a bottle of Barbera del Monferrato Frizzante, don't be surprised if your dark red wine comes out a little bubbly. One of the few red wines that can be made sparkling, Barbera is full of surprises. Unlike the Italians, who are consistent in their excellent taste.

I say it's time to pay attention to *all* the wine offerings of Italy, not just the dominating Barolos and Chiantis. Who knows? Barbera could be the perfect drinkable red you've been looking for. And all this time it's been right under your nose, in the foothills of northern Italy, hiding under Nebbiolo's shadow.

THE TASTING

THE BOTTLE: *Michele Chiarlo Le Orme Barbera d'Asti 2017. Piedmont, Italy, $13.*

As expected, the wine is dark. Borderline purple dark. Anyone who's tried more than, say, five red wines, may know the old adage that the darker the wine, the more intense the flavor. But, as we know already, Barbera is trickier than that.

At first sniff, there are notes of raspberry, cherry, and a bit of perfume. Not Chanel No. 5—a scent reserved for people as old as the fashion house itself. No, the perfume is more subtle. And less musty.

The flavor is full of cherries. A bright red cherry that's more tart than sweet. And, the surprising grape that Barbera is, it's not as tannic (mouth-drying) as one would expect from a wine so dark. But it is zippy and acidic. Overall, it's still very drinkable. So much so that you could have this on the table during the summer months and no one would so much as bat an eye. A rare feat for a red wine, in my opinion.

Barbera is full of bright red cherry coupled with lip-smacking acidity and as light as a Beaujolais (more on her later). Quite the impressive little Italian grape. Look out, light and drinkable Chianti, Barbera has stepped into the ring.

IN THE WILD

Barbera is a wine you'd drink while sitting on a balcony or patio at sunset during the summer. You're enjoying charcuterie and having a classy-yet-informal catch up with your favorite group of friends. The whole set-up makes you feel effortlessly chic. Not only are you having red wine outside like a European, but it's a delight to drink. Plus, you've opened a wine that's decidedly Not Another Rosé. How worldly of you.

Your friends who tend toward the Big, Bad Reds (Merlot, Malbec, Syrah), will appreciate Barbera's fruit and acidity. And those who don't enjoy overpowering red wines will take comfort in how light-bodied it is. But no matter who is there to enjoy it, know that the Italians call Barbera an "everyday drinking wine," so you can't go wrong. Besides, no one is in a position to argue with the country that invented *la dolce vita*.

BORDEAUX BLEND

To find a French bottle, look in: Bordeaux!

THERE ARE ONLY TWO WINES that come to mind when anyone says "French red wine:" Burgundy and Bordeaux. Classically named for where they're grown and not for their grapes, Burgundy and Bordeaux are the prototype for excellence in the (old) world of red wine. It's almost impossible to find a book or documentary on wine that doesn't talk up either of the two. But truth be told, Bordeaux is the front-runner and has been for millennia.

Known for being more tannic and bold in flavor, the red wines from Bordeaux are suited well for blending—the process in which winemakers combine different varieties of wine or wine grapes in a single bottle. But make no mistake, rigorous standards ensure that each individual grape in a blend is still excellent on its own. While most often made from Cabernet Sauvignon and Merlot grapes from the region, Bordeaux blends can also include Cabernet Franc, Malbec, Petit Verdot, and even Carménère. Regardless of what's in the blend, each grape needs to be perfect.

The region is unyielding in its traditional standards, known for producing some of the world's most sought-after red wines. Châteaus Lafite, Latour, and Haut-Brion—all Bordeaux, all legendary—warrant an average price tag of $900 per bottle. Should you want a notable vintage from the Big Three, expect to pay tens of thousands per bottle for the privilege. With classic red wines, the choice is obvious and ironclad. If you want a taste of time-honored French prestige, Bordeaux is the only place you need to look.

THE TASTING

THE BOTTLE: *Château Lilian Ladouys Saint-Estephe 2016. Bordeaux, France. $27.*

An opened bottle of Bordeaux is smelled before it's seen. Case in point: the scent of overpowering fruit seeps out of the bottle the minute you pull the cork. Dare to stick your nose *in* your glass, and you'll be met with blackberry juice, brandy, vanilla, and nostril-singing alcohol. Couple that with the appearance of garnet-colored cough syrup, and you have a perfect first impression of Bordeaux. Audacious, yes. Off-putting, not yet.

The heaviness of the Bordeaux confirms itself the minute you take a sip. It all but takes a nap in your mouth while drying out every taste bud it can find. Make no mistake, the tannins aren't shy in France. But the dominance of the blackberries-soaked-in-pomegranate-juice flavors help balance out the mouth-drying effects. Let it linger on your palate, and the flavor doesn't stop there. No, there's dried herbs—sage, thyme—and a surprising note of graphite—as though you'd licked a freshly sharpened yellow pencil. The kind that got destroyed by the wall-mounted sharpeners in your third-grade classroom. It's a lot to handle, and being French, it won't make any apologies. This wine is juicy, herbaceous, and solemnly dense. A classic French Bordeaux, indeed.

IN THE WILD

Bordeaux is a wine that warrants an intellectual setting. Or at least a setting that pretends to be. In fact, it would be well-suited to a rich friend's high-ceilinged library, filled with books that haven't been touched, let alone opened. Eventually, inspired by the classic literature on the shelves, someone might suggest smoking cigars. Because that's what lavish private libraries are for.

Or, on the off-chance that you have no rich friend, a rough day could warrant a glass, too. A day so insufferable that you're desperate for a comfortable couch and an hour of solitude. After all, a French Bordeaux is heavy and demanding, so it can stand up to that rough day just fine.

CABERNET FRANC

*To find a French bottle, look in: the Loire (Chinon,
Bourgueil, St.-Nicolas-de-Bourgueil)*

THE FIRST CABERNET ONE USUALLY thinks of is rarely
the Franc and almost always the Sauvignon. But you can't have
the second without the first. In fact, Cabernet Franc is a parent
grape of Cabernet Sauvignon (the other parent being Sauvignon
Blanc), meaning that the Cab Sauv you love wouldn't be here if
it weren't cross-bred by the two. Even so, people rarely choose
Cabernet Franc over Cabernet Sauvignon. And if they do, it's
usually only as a component of a red wine blend. Never a solo
star.

There's a reason Cabernet Franc is rarely drunk on its own.
Time after time, it takes a backseat to its own kin because it's

lower in tannins, body, alcohol, and color. Most red wine drinkers seek adventure when they sit down with a red wine, so they lean towards the more robust Malbecs or Cab Sauvs. Don't believe me? When was the last time you encountered someone ordering a light-bodied Grenache or Beaujolais at dinner? Big and bold is the preference of many red wine drinkers.

But the world of lighter-bodied reds is not all bad. The more people develop their palates, the more wines they're willing to explore. Plus, there comes a time in every Cab Sauv lover's life when they face the opportunity to meet its maker. Franc-ly, I don't see why they wouldn't want to. The Cabernet Sauvignon wouldn't be half the grape it is without Cab Franc. Besides, the apple/grape doesn't fall too far from the tree/vine.

THE TASTING

THE BOTTLE: *Domaine de la Chanteleuserie Bourgueil Alouettes 2018. Loire Valley, France. $18.*

Cabernet Franc is more of a medium-bodied red wine. It might not be heavy enough to take a nap in your mouth like a Bordeaux, but it certainly won't knock itself back. In the glass, it smells like cherry liqueur. You know, the kind you used to steal from your parents' liquor cabinet when you were young and didn't know any better. There are also surprising notes of hot rubber in the mix, as well as chopped green bell pepper. The aromas are all over the place, yes, and much more herbaceous than its Cab Sauv lovechild.

When you taste it, the fruit isn't dominant. A slow-ripening grape, Cabernet Franc rarely matures to full-ripeness before harvesting. This lack of maturation on the grape's part usually means that its wine won't be chock-full of ripe fruity flavor . So instead of fruit, there's essence of hot tar mixed with a medicinal, chalky, cherry lozenge. Quite the unique flavor profile. If you're into those flavors, that is.

This Cab Franc is also bitter, but not overwhelming. Evidence of tannins, yes, but not completely overpowering. For fervent Francophiles, it's a perfect representation of a French red wine. Nothing ripe, fruity, or warm about it. Except for the tar, of course.

IN THE WILD

Cab Franc from the Loire Valley is an intellectual with a dry sense of humor. A black- or tortoiseshell-framed glasses wearer who lives vicariously through classic literature. And definitely an introvert who doesn't look to try new things for the sake of novelty. You know the type. A straight shooter. An academic. The one who delivers their rare opinion bluntly, because they don't know any other way to do it.

That's what Cabernet Franc is. It's alarming in its straightforward nature. Not fruity, not savory, but earthy. And there's no mistaking it. It tells you what you've signed up for on the first sip, and all at once. It's a very "take it or leave it" kind of wine. It won't be fruity to appease the palate. It won't be smoky to stand out. It's French to the core and won't pretend to be something it's not. Even if it's the forgotten-about parent of the most popular red wine in the world, Cab Franc doesn't care. And for that, it deserves our respect. Carry on, Cab Franc, carry on.

CABERNET SAUVIGNON

To find a French bottle, look in: Bordeaux (Margaux, St.-Julien, Pauillac, St.-Estephe, Pessac-Léognan, Listrac, Moulis) and Languedoc-Roussillon (varietally named Vin de Pays d'Oc)

AH, YES. THE *REAL* CABERNET. The Cab heard round the world: Cabernet Sauvignon. The go-to red wine at a steakhouse, at a dinner party, as a gift, as a must-taste stop on a wine tour. Cabernet Sauvignon is everywhere, on everyone's lips the moment you ask "red or white?" It's planted all over the world and more often than not, thrives in any condition. From Canada, to South Africa, and everywhere in between, Cabernet Sauvignon grows. But for whatever reason, we're told that *the best* Cabs come from California or France. Which makes sense: Cabernet Sauvignon was one of two California wines that beat out the French in the Judgment of Paris (1976)—the most famous blind tasting in the world. At the time, France was the region to beat, and California a nobody. And yet, the results stood. California's victory heralded a new era, one in which Napa was a key player in the wine producing world. But Cabernet Sauvignon is the most popular grape *in the world.* Doesn't the world reach beyond California and France?

Here's the thing. If my search for a good Cab Sauv had ended with California and France, I would not be a fan. Never have I ever been impressed by a Cabernet from California, yet I adore other Californian wines. Many love France's historically esteemed bottles, yet their red wines don't resonate with me. So, what's a girl to do? Give up on the World's Greatest Red altogether? Or should I look elsewhere, miles away, to find a Cab that can stand on its own? Taste is subjective, and Cabernet Sauvignon is no exception. When the notable regions don't speak to your palate, there are plenty of others to explore. And that's exactly how Chile saved Cabernet Sauvignon for me.

THE TASTING

THE BOTTLE: *Los Vascos Cabernet Sauvignon 2017. Colchagua, Chile. $9.*

This wine is a steal for two reasons. One, it's $9 and doesn't taste like dirty, stale grape juice. Two, Los Vascos is a South American estate extension of the Lafite chateau in Bordeaux. Lafite is one of a few French wineries that regularly garners a price tag of $900 for their bottles of red. The fact that they've extended their prestigious way of wine-making to Los Vascos is worth noting. *Because this bottle is $9.* You don't usually get wine made under the umbrella of one of the most prestigious producers in the world for just $9. But reputation only gets you so far. What matters is how the bottle tastes.

Any good tasting starts, paradoxically, with smell. And this wine's aromas are not what anyone familiar with "the best" Cabernets would expect. It's full of blackberry, blueberry, subtle notes of vanilla, and fresh, earthy sage.

In taste, it's black cherry, blackberry, and cassis (blackcurrant). The mouth-drying tannin is there, but the effect is very mild. In fact, the tannins don't linger at all. All you're left with is a smooth and syrupy finish à la crème de cassis, unlike California Cabs, which leave behind a lingering taste of tobacco and pencil lead, or the French Cabs, with black licorice and plum flavors.

Chilean Cabernet offers a well-rounded taste. It's not as full-bodied as a Cab from France or California, but you still get a nice depth of flavor. Once you're done tasting, you're left wanting more. Look out, France and California, Chile has arrived.

IN THE WILD

Chilean Cabernet Sauvignon is the perfect wine to bring if you're meeting your significant other's parents for the first time. Perfect because, for whatever reason, dads *love* Cabernets from California. They've probably all had a bottle at a steakhouse for a business meeting and decided it was their go-to wine from then on out.

So, being the worldly adult that you are, you'd bring him this bottle from Chile and get points right off the bat. It's delicious, it's a Cab, and it's intriguingly not French or Californian. Bonus points if you'll also be having a summer cookout. Not only will he like the wine as a standalone, but it'll be a perfect match for his grilled steak. It's fool-proof.

Or, should you find yourself surrounded by wine snobs, this wine will also come in handy. You know the types: "I only drink wines from the Old World—you can't match the tradition." Or: "You can't find a good bottle of Chardonnay outside of Chablis—you just can't." Or the true contrarians: "Lafite is *so* overrated." These are the people who think they're God's gift to wine commentary. They went on a winery tour in Bordeaux four years ago and won't shut up about it. So now, they think they've earned the right to snub any wine not from France.

These are the same people who no doubt brag about spending a grand on a bottle from the noble Bordeaux chateaus. But you know better. You know that a bottle of Los Vascos is made under the Lafite name. And it only costs $9. So, you can give them this pearl of wisdom and watch their reactions. Or you can just keep it to yourself and find a new crowd to drink with. Either way, I won't judge.

GAMAY

To find a French bottle, look in: Beaujolais

GAMAY IS A GRAPE YOU'VE definitely come across, just under a different name. And chances are if you've seen every episode of *Sex and the City*, like I have, the name "Beaujolais" rings a bell. Once upon a New York time, Samantha Jones was the best female character on TV. The candid, one-liner queen of the hit HBO show declared that finding yourself in a dilemma was "like getting a bad bottle of Beaujolais Nouveau the first day of season." I never knew what she was talking about. It evaded me for years. Until one day, on a wine spree in Binny's, my local wine superstore, I realized that Beaujolais Nouveau is a wine made in, wait for it, Beaujolais, France (quelle surprise). The region is best known for growing 75% of the world's

Gamay grapes. So, thank you, Samantha Jones, for illuminating Beaujolais for the rest of us. It's a Burgundian red wine worth paying attention to.

Now, in terms of quality, "Beaujolais" and "Beaujolais Nouveau" are your entry-level wines. Above those are the "Villages" and "Cru" levels—with "Cru" being the highest. No offense to Samantha, but with her generous PR salary and apartment in the Meatpacking District, I'd imagine she'd *at least* spring for the Beaujolais Villages. But hey, who am I to judge the queen of New York circa 1996? I didn't even know what a Beaujolais was. But I do now.

THE TASTING

THE BOTTLE: *Louis Jadot Beaujolais-Villages 2017. Burgundy, France. $13.*

Knowing this wine would be full of fruit (lighter red wines usually are), the aroma of raspberries, cherries and the slightest hint of nutmeg comes as no surprise. It's a juicy-smelling wine, the likes of which mirror Pinot Noir from California. And it's easy to swirl in the glass—no heavy tannins here.

Beaujolais Villages tastes like cran-raspberry juice with hints of dirt and a tongue coating of ripe banana and rose petals. It has more flavor than you might expect from an innocent, light red wine. It's also more acidic than you'd think. Louis Jadot makes you want to smack your lips like Michael Scott did drinking scotch at David Wallace's house before asking for some Splenda. But don't let that deter you. It's still a pleasantly juicy tasting experience.

The overall profile is of red fruit mixed with rose petal, brown banana, a hint of dirt, all zipped up with bright acidity. It's a lot, but somehow it works. French wines always do, with not a flavor out of place.

IN THE WILD

Much like its unofficial ambassador, Samantha Jones, Beaujolais doesn't take itself too seriously. Yeah, sure, there's a lot going on, but it's all wrapped up in a fun, flirty package. It's endearing and feminine, yet maintains an edge to keep you coming back for more. And despite being a French wine, Beaujolais is laid-back. Drinks before dinner kind of laid-back. Much more approachable than you'd expect looking at the label, which screams Old World French class.

Still, Beaujolais' nature serves as a great segue for anyone hesitant to dabble in red wines. It's light, fruity, and acidic enough to make the transition into reds tolerable. Unless, of course, you get a bad bottle of Beaujolais Nouveau the first day of season. Samantha Jones would never.

GRENACHE

SPANISH WINES AND I GO way back. My first wine experience was when I was 16 years old on a school trip to Spain. Night one, I tried my first ~~glass~~ glasses of sangria. Unsurprisingly, I enjoyed it so much that it became a dinner staple every night we were there. I'm still unclear on how a bunch of teenagers got away with openly drinking on a school trip. I guess our chaperones considered it an important cultural experience. Regardless, that first sip ushered me into the world of wine at the ripe young age of under-18. Ever since, Spanish wines have always had a special place in my heart.

And apparently, I'm not the only one. Sangria is so popular that there have been endless recipe variations throughout the world since the 1960s. Cool, but who cares about Sangria, right? We're talking about Grenache. Well, it turns out that this beloved, fruit-and-wine cocktail—the exact elixir that taught me what it meant to be drunk at 16—is traditionally made with Grenache wine. Or as Spain calls it, Garnacha.

Garnacha lends itself perfectly to the infamous Spanish cocktail. Sampling it alone, you'll quickly see how this wine can transform. Add in some brandy and fruit, and suddenly Garnacha has flowered into Sangria. To love Sangria is to love Garnacha, whether you know it yet or not. And tasting it as a standalone is never a mistake.

THE TASTING

THE BOTTLE: *Zestos Old Vine Garnacha 2018. Madrid, Spain. $12.*

As the core ingredient of highly-drinkable Sangria, one can expect Garnacha to exhibit ample red fruit, both in taste and in smell. In this bottle, there's a plethora of red fruit aromas—specifically, dried cherries and raspberries. The smell is light, but not watery. Juicy, but not syrupy.

And it tastes exactly as expected: juicy red fruits, a touch of leather, and a hint of spice at the end to keep it from resembling actual juice. It's light in the mouth and doesn't linger on your palate very long, making it a very drinkable wine. Garnacha is also acidic, but not nearly as zippy as the

Italian Barbera or the French Beaujolais. It's a liquid representation of a Spanish flamenco: vibrant, enjoyable, and fluid, with just enough European elegance to remind you you're not drinking wine out of a plastic bag.

IN THE WILD

You're sitting down for a sunset dinner outside on a balcony, patio, or sidewalk seating. Having enjoyed a languid day sunning at the beach, you're tired from the heat and blissfully unaware of your impending sunburn. Dried out and hungry for seafood, you order a Garnacha and grilled octopus. "It's too hot for red wine," says your dinner companion. "Not for Garnacha," you insist.

The wine arrives, followed by your grilled entrée. You take a sip; it's lovely. Bountiful, bright red fruit, coupled with the slightest edge of leather and spice to keep it interesting. Paired with the charred, briny octopus, it dances. The cherries balancing the char. The acid complementing the brine. The Garnacha is summer-proof. This year-round red makes a name for itself alongside any outdoor dining excursion full of seafood and tapas, the way Spain intended.

GSM/RHÔNE BLEND

To find a French bottle, look in: the southern Rhône (Châteauneuf-du-Pape, Gigondas, Vacqueyras, Rasteau, Côtes du Rhône) and Languedoc-Roussillon (Corbières, Faugères, Minervois, St.-Chinian, La Clape, Montpeyroux, Pic Saint Loup, Quatourze, St.-Saturnin)

THE GRENACHE, SYRAH, AND MOURVEDRE grapes form the base of most red wine blends from the Southern Rhône region in France. Call it GSM, call it Côtes du Rhône—it's all the same in style, but can vary in flavor depending on how each winery wishes to balance the three GSM grapes.

Grenache is the lightest of the three, very red fruit dominant with a hint of baking spice, and highly drinkable, as we've recently discovered. In France, this grape usually makes up the bulk of any GSM/Rhône blend. Syrah, however, is much darker. Full of dark berries, savory black licorice or olive flavor, and occasionally aromas of bacon fat, this grape adds serious depth and boldness to the blend. Mourvèdre (a.k.a. Monastrell), like Syrah, is also a bold, savory grape. But unique to it are its signature smoky flavor and mouth-gripping tannins.

So, it's easy to see how a GSM blend can be drastically different from one winery to the next, depending on the balance of each distinct grape. But that's what's fun about it. These blends are as unique as snowflakes, especially considering the fact that they're produced around the world. Blend variations, climate differences, weather changes—all the elements add up to a unique taste every time you sit down with a bottle. Which makes it a hard wine to write off altogether. You're bound to encounter a region, a winery, a vintage that you like. It's impossible not to. Why else would GSM also stand for "Get Some More," if it weren't so widely appealing? Sure, I made that up, but it doesn't make it any less true.

THE TASTING

THE BOTTLE: *Hahn Winery GSM 2018. Monterey, California. $13.*

This bottle from Hahn smells like raspberries, black cherries, and an overwhelming whiff of alcohol, which leads me to believe that Grenache, the boozier, fruitier grape of the three, is dominant here. The wine is richly colored, more of a purplish-red, thanks to the blending of the darker grapes (Syrah and Mourvèdre), and heavy in thickness. The wine-proficient among us would say this wine has "legs," meaning that it leaves behind thick tear drops after you swirl it in the glass.

At first, it tastes like a park on the Fourth of July: like sparklers and bug spray. But if you let it breathe for a few minutes, a more pronounced berry flavor comes through; among them, notes of new car leather and the flavor of how a just-lit match smells. Plus, a dusting of cinnamon.

There are so many flavors to explore within a GSM, and this Californian variety is no different. The boldness of the 'S' and 'M' grapes, responsible for the leather and cedar flavors, shine through, making it easy to see why blending them with a lighter, fruitier, more acidic grape like Grenache makes for a fun blend. The berry fruit and the savory, leathery spiciness complement each other in the end, making it quite delectable.

Initially, it's hard to see how these three distinct grapes can mingle well without one overpowering the others. But sample enough of the GSM, or Côtes du Rhône, and the flavors will surprise you every time with their balance, flavor, and body.

IN THE WILD

GSM is a very masculine wine, which feels slightly wrong to say after my dad practically spit it out, but I said what I said. It's a beefy wine that needs a strong meal to go with it. Think aged cheddar, smoked meats, brown butter and sage. Anything dominant and bold in flavor would be the ideal match for a GSM.

It also needs a strong personality to truly enjoy it. The Syrah and Mourvèdre grapes take no prisoners. They're smoky, tannic, and oftentimes savory. So if you have a cigar-smoking uncle with a deep, baritone voice whose laugh can be heard for miles, and who also has an affinity for porterhouse steaks, he'd be the ideal company to share a Rhône blend with. Bold, effusive, and smoky, they'd be like two peas in a French pod.

MALBEC

MALBEC IS QUITE THE INTRIGUING grape. Maybe it's the opaque purplish hue. Or that it leaves a unique, magenta-colored rim when you pour it into a glass. Whatever it is, Malbec's intrigue and reputation as a fantastic red wine never would have reached the world if it weren't for its relocation to Argentina.

Originally, Malbec grew in France, but it was so susceptible to disease and decay that winemakers invested less and less growing space to it. They couldn't devote their valuable soil to a grape that failed more than it prospered. That is, until some astute Argentinians thought to take some roots back to Mendoza, betting that the destitute grape needed a change of scenery. Lo and behold, the Malbec grape thrived south of the equator. Yet, it wasn't until the early 2000s, when wine prices in Europe became too high, that Malbec got its chance to shine internationally.

Luckily, Malbec grown in Argentina is so drinkable and affordable that word of mouth spread the grape like wildfire. We now have a beautifully bold red wine at our disposal, thanks to the ingenuity of a select few Argentinian winemakers. And after a sip, you'll see that it's in a league of its own.

THE TASTING

THE BOTTLE: *Crios de Susana Balbo Malbec 2018. Mendoza, Argentina. $12.*

Malbec is so worldly and sophisticated that its color in the glass is actually *royal purple*. You'll never encounter another wine with Malbec's unique magenta rim. The wine is opaque, dark, and smells incredibly of juice. Pouring out of the glass are aromas of ripe red fruit (almost like a strawberry fruit snack) and of some flower whose scent you can only smell when you get close to it—a violet, maybe.

Unfortunately, the wine doesn't taste like a strawberry fruit snack. It errs on the side of black cherries, baking spices, dirt, and bittersweet cocoa powder. The tannins are there, as well as the slightest bit of acidity, which I imagine will fade as the bottle ages—big red wines rarely keep their youthful acidity.

The Crios Malbec is big enough that it coats the back of your throat, making it very unappealing to guzzle. Perhaps the Malbec is trying to force you to sip it slowly. Or maybe its structure is its way of commanding respect. After all, it *is* dressed in royal purple.

IN THE WILD

Malbec is a culturally refined world traveler, never one to settle where it won't thrive. A grape that knows what it wants, what it needs, and refuses to change for anybody. Malbec is the embodiment of worldliness, sophistication, and depth. It's always trying to reveal to you new things, encourage you to explore, and tap into your deepest thoughts. But it's far from snobby. Malbec is approachable, yet respectable. Enjoyable, but not shoddy. Regal, yet down to earth. It captures the balance of sophistication and approachability exceptionally well.

The mature cherry, the bittersweet cocoa, the baking spices all work together to achieve a unique flavor delivered in a refined package. Malbec achieves what many wines only strive to: it's impressive without trying too hard to be. And who can't appreciate that?

MERLOT

To find a French bottle, look in: Bordeaux (Pomerol, St.-Émilion, Fronsac, Canon-Fronsac, the Côtes) and Languedoc-Roussillon (varietally named Vin de Pays d'Oc)

MERLOT IS THE SECOND MOST popular wine in the United States, behind Cabernet Sauvignon, with whom it also shares a parent grape. Both Cabernet Sauvignon and Merlot were fathered by the Cabernet Franc grape. Merlot's mom is Magdeleine Noire des Charentes, a rare grape almost lost to extinction ten years ago. But, thanks to a few pioneers in southwest France, the Magdeleine has a fighting chance at coming back. As long as we keep seeking out wines we've never heard of, we'll always have a variety of grapes to enjoy, blend, and breed, one of the best 'bred' wines being Merlot.

Merlot is not an easy grape to grow, which, unfortunately, means its wines are easy to make poorly. The worst-made Merlots taste like tannins, alcohol, and not much else. But, when grown properly, Merlot adapts to its soil, bringing out beautiful flavor every time. Some people won't agree, and I can almost guarantee that those people's opinions originated with the cult-classic movie *Sideways*.

In the movie, Paul Giamatti's character, a self-described wine aficionado, hates Merlot. So much so that one of the most famous lines in the whole movie is when he announces: "If anyone orders Merlot, I'm leaving. I am not drinking any f***ing Merlot." After the movie's release, there was, in fact, a notable dent in Merlot sales—the correlation between the two still wildly up for debate. But like any other wine, Merlot can be made terribly as well as beautifully. To find an excellent one, you just have to go where the top-notch grapes grow: Bordeaux and California.

THE TASTING

THE BOTTLE: *Alexander Valley Vineyards Merlot 2016. Sonoma County, California. $19.*

Knowing at this point that France's red wines are not my speed, I opted for California instead. The North Coast (encompassing the well-known wine regions of Napa and Sonoma) is a key player in the world of Merlot, regularly producing grapes of value. But don't try to undercut the market too much—$10 won't be enough to get you a worthy bottle.

Pour a glass of the Alexander Valley and, instantly, you smell black cherry, leather, and... a hint of household cleaner? It's eucalyptus, with its unmistakable minty-pine scent.

Taste-wise, this wine is enjoyably predictable. It's like a black cherry lozenge mixed with super-bittersweet chocolate. Think 85-90% cacao-level of bittersweet. And a hint of sage. But the finish is smooth. The tannins, however, are not—they coat your entire mouth. It's like accidentally yawning in the middle of the Sahara Desert. But, if you can tolerate a heavy hand of mouth-drying tannin, the flavors are worth enduring. The black cherry, the bitter cocoa, the hint of sage are all wrapped up in a smoothly-balanced finish, with a vacuum of tannin bringing up the rear.

Merlot is *voluptuous*. The flavors are rich, the wine itself is heavy, and there's no aspect of it that doesn't coat your entire mouth. It's a heavy-hitter, and luckily, making a comeback (sorry, Paul).

IN THE WILD

Merlot is a moth to the flame of an existential crisis. It's big and heavy enough to handle the weight of life's problems, yet smooth enough to keep you from despairing. It won't sugarcoat, it won't soothe, but it has enough depth and just enough comfort in its berry flavors to carry you through.

Plus, Merlot has been through some things on its own. Its reputation has been tarnished, it's been unfairly discriminated against, and so many people produce it in a way that doesn't measure up to its promise. Merlot knows denial, which makes it a perfect comrade for commiseration. But if you can just get to the other side (of a good bottle), you'll be enlightened about its beautiful potential.

MONTEPULCIANO

THE NAMES OF ITALIAN WINES are always fun to rattle off in mixed company: *Sangiovese, Brachetto, Barolo, Montepulciano.* They instantly make you feel more cultured, European, and well-traveled—even if you've never heard of the wine you're enthusiastically enunciating. Montepulciano isn't an Italian wine often heard of or seen on a wine list, but it ranks as Italy's second-most exported grape (after Sangiovese, the grape responsible for Chianti), so it must have some international appeal.

Like Merlot, Montepulciano often falls victim to low-quality production, since it's grown so widely across Abruzzo. But just because it's easy to find a shoddy variety doesn't mean you can't or won't find a robust, drinkable bottle—especially if you look in Teramo, a province within the Abruzzo region. There, unforgiving soil surprisingly brings out the best in the Montepulciano grape—its tannins, acidity, and dark berry flavor.

Unlike other reds, which can blend and bend to transform into a variety of flavors and styles, Montepulciano thrives as it is—a dry Italian red table wine. Should you tire of the same old Chianti, or want an age-worthy Italian wine you've probably never heard of, Montepulciano can sub in nicely.

THE TASTING

THE BOTTLE: *Antonio & Elio Monti Montepulciano d'Abruzzo 2013. Abruzzo, Italy. $12.*

Montepulciano smells ominous, the bold berry flavors pouring out of the glass. It's dripping with punchy blackberries and tart juicy cherries. It's also savory-smelling, with hints of plastic pool toy, the likes of which I haven't smelled since my last encounter with a Washington Riesling.

As for the taste, it's a smorgasbord of flavor. There's subdued black fruit, a hint of black licorice, black pepper, and smoke, all wrapped in notable tannins. Not to worry—the tannins and the acidity balance each other out to keep the other from becoming too powerful. It's intimidating, bold, and full of savory, dark flavors. The blackberry, the smoke, the licorice all mingle together while drying out your mouth ever so slightly. And yet, the acidity makes the Montepulciano juicy, too. It's a lot. While the Barbera is Italy's friendly red guzzler, the Montepulciano is Italy's savory powerhouse. You can't help but respect it.

IN THE WILD

Montepulciano is an intimidating, big-boned, Italian uncle who cooks for people and always gets positive feedback. Probably because you'd *never* tell him you didn't like what he cooked for you to his face, even if it tasted like herbs and plastic. Montepulciano commands respect that way. In a sense, it's the Italian counterpart to a French Bordeaux. It's bold, intense, and a little savory. And it doesn't care what you think either way.

But it's still very lovable, especially alongside any red-sauce Italian dish. A big Montepulciano is ideal for dishes centered around smoky, spicy sausage. And honestly, I think it would be offended if it *weren't* included at dinner. Forget drinking alone, Italian wines like this belong right next to Mama's famous Italian sausage. It's only polite.

NEBBIOLO

BAROLO AND BARBARESCO ARE BOTH famous wines produced from the Nebbiolo grape, to which I'm thankfully no stranger. In fact, last year for my birthday I received three bottles of Barolo from three different (and wildly generous) people. Once you become fascinated with wine, you become very easy to shop for, I guess. But even prior to my three-Barolo-birthday, my first encounter with the wine is something I still remember, clear as day.

Early in my tasting expedition, I learned that Barolos are not only highly revered but highly expensive. The Nebbiolo grape is high-maintenance, grown almost exclusively on the hills of Piedmont, making it somewhat of a luxury. In fact, when you find yourself in the company of this prestigious grape, you rarely have a lackluster taste.

Knowing this, and being in my twenties, I knew I could never in good conscience afford a bottle myself—or risk shelling out $17 for a glass. Luckily, a good friend knew a sommelier and beverage director at one of the trendiest restaurants in Chicago. He graciously offered us both a taste.

Believe me when I tell you that that glass of Barolo changed the way I viewed red wines. It was savory, smooth, and full of flavor, yet it was as light as Pinot. It was sensational. And it enlightened me as to why spending $40+ on a bottle of wine can absolutely be worth it. Nebbiolo's reputation for producing exceptional red wine, in a very specific corner of Italy, and only under the exact right circumstances and soil, is honorable. The prime definition of high-risk, high-reward, the byproducts of Nebbiolo are two of the world's most celebrated red wines year in, year out.

THE TASTING

THE BOTTLE: *Renato Ratti Ochetti Nebbiolo 2015. Piedmont, Italy. $22.*

Having been blessed with a handful of opportunities to sample Barolos in the $40-50 price range (as gracious gifts), it became necessary to see what a basic Nebbiolo wine offered at a more wallet-friendly price point. Especially because my own money was on the line this time.

The aromas of this Renato are on par with its more expensive siblings: pulverized cherries, black licorice candy, and earthy clay. Nebbiolo often smells like red fruit, earth, and sometimes leather, so it's comforting to know that the aromas seem to be consistent across the board.

The taste is a mouthful of sour cherry, toasted almond, a very faint hint of vanilla, and a pinch of petroleum. Emphasis on "mouthful", because Nebbiolo is almost always overwhelming, being full to the brim of both tannin and acidity, a combo rarely seen in red wines, and one that's unique to Nebbiolo. It's punchy. It's acidic. And it's heavy.

A powerhouse red no matter what you spend, Nebbiolo has a reputation that won't stop being upheld. Barolo, Barbaresco, or a simple Nebbiolo will offer a taste unlike any other red you'll encounter. Try it and tell me otherwise.

IN THE WILD

You're at a dimly lit, probably Michelin-starred restaurant for a business dinner. There are men in suits at every turn, and the sounds of Very Important People having Very Important Dinners fill every corner. The wine list is presented, and based on your boss's penchant for ordering the most expensive cut of meat on the menu, it would be impossible to imagine dinner without a Big, Bold, Red. He requests a bottle of Barolo, expecting you to nod approvingly. "Excellent choice, sir."

It's a predictable order—those with fat wallets and an equally large desire to be seen in an impressive light always reach for it. It's expensive, it's revered, it screams "look at me, I have excellent taste." And while Barolo is, in fact, a wine of excellent taste, the attempt at appearing impressive is thinly veiled. Add in an order of anything with black truffles involved, and the intention is clear. So, soak up the praise, bask in the flavors, and remember that a Barolo can't buy you love. Just an exceptional tasting experience.

PINOT NOIR

To find a French bottle, look in: Burgundy and its
villages Côte de Nuits (Chambertin, Marsannay, Morey,
Musigny), Côte de Beaune (Pommard, Volnay, Santenay),
Côte Chalonnaise (Mercurey, Givry); and Alsace

PEOPLE *ADORE* PINOT NOIR. IT'S romanticized at every turn. And it's not hard to see why. Known for its dominant red fruit flavors and lightweight body, it's hard to find anything disagreeable about it. It's so front-of-mind for wine drinkers that it even has its own holiday—Pinot Noir Day falls on August 18th. To say people adore it might even be an understatement.

However, Pinot Noir is a notoriously fussy grape, making finding a great bottle a true treasure hunt. But once you find one, you can't help but rave. Even among the most middle-of-the road tastes, Pinot Noir is a crowd-pleaser. Appealing both to white wine drinkers with its lighter body and minimal tannins and red wine drinkers with its rich, fruity flavor, Pinot pleases. Luckily, this widely appealing, yet high-maintenance grape is made well outside of Burgundy, too. Just ask the panel enlisted for the *Somm 3* documentary.

The idea behind *Somm 3* was to recreate the infamous 1976 Judgment of Paris. An original *Somm* cast member, Dustin, set out to prove that France wasn't the only region making top quality Pinot Noir. In a blind tasting of six different Pinots, made from six different vineyards around the world, the judges (a smorgasbord of unique wine personalities) were to choose a favorite based on flavor alone. Try as they might to pick out the Burgundian varieties, the first-place winner ended up being a Pinot from Santa Barbara, California. Just like in 1976, California proved that it could beat out France in making Chardonnay, Cabernet Sauvignon, and now... Pinot Noir. And luckily, you can get a great bottle from California for less than a great bottle from Burgundy—no flavor spared.

THE TASTING

THE BOTTLE: *Coppola Diamond Collection Pinot Noir Silver Label 2017. Monterey, California. $14.*

Appealing before you even take your first sip, Pinot Noir from California smells lovely, with notes of raspberries, hot gravel, and red rose petals. With a light and juicy aroma, it's destined to be very drinkable, like all the lighter reds before it. Distinct and delicate.

Notoriously red-fruit dominant, this Pinot has more of a mulled strawberry taste, with red plums and allspice. Actually, the flavor is well-suited for splashing in to a homemade batch of red fruit jam, the acidity and palatable fruits helping deepen the fruity flavor of the jam.

Before I started tasting, I looked up the flavors of California Pinot Noirs and all my sources agreed: allspice was inescapable. But, I'll be honest—I hadn't the slightest clue what allspice tasted like. Not wanting to stunt my flavor acumen, I went into the pantry, dipped my finger in a jar of allspice and had myself a taste. And wouldn't you know it, allspice is *exactly* the flavor that sticks out in this bottle. Due diligence in wine tasting is ridiculous and yet clearly necessary. The cost of knowledge being, at worst, a briefly off-beat moment.

Pinot Noir makes you do unusual things, but that's its charm, I guess. Wooing drinkers with its bountiful strawberry flavor and keeping you hooked with its highly drinkable lightness, Pinot is absolutely the wine of the people.

IN THE WILD

Pinot Noir from California is that friend who always looks out for others, never straying from their post. They possess the best qualities one can hope for in a friend: affable, engaging, and loved by many. Sure, they can be fussy sometimes. But Pinot's core is solid gold. Even amidst the high praise, it still tries to be the best version of itself it can be: a grape delighting people all over the world.

It's endearing, really, sitting down with a Pinot. Baring its soul, it begs you to feel welcomed, pacified, and treated to a wonderful flavor experience. And Pinot Noir makes sure it keeps no secrets. It wants you to enjoy it. And, for that, it's a very respectable grape, indeed.

SANGIOVESE

SANGIOVESE IS THE ITALIAN GRAPE with many names: Chianti, Brunello, "Super Tuscan." Whatever the name, the Sangiovese grape is Tuscany's pride and joy. It's so prevalent across Tuscany and the rest of the country that Chianti is known collectively as Italy's table wine. Walk into an authentic Italian restaurant and you'll see it. Whether painted on the wall, on the menu, or on your table, there'll undoubtedly be a bottle of Chianti sitting in a straw basket, known as a *fiasco*. There's even a small mural of a bottle of Chianti, fiasco and all, on a dining room wall at my parents' house. My mom doesn't even drink wine, so what does that tell you?

That's the thing about Tuscany; it lures you in. Diane Lane couldn't stay away. Julia Roberts spent one third of her *Eat, Pray, Love* pilgrimage there. Unspoken or not, Italy is always calling. And Sangiovese is the necessary small talk. If we're to answer the call of historically romantic villas, impeccably divine food, and the charismatic whims of Italian fate, Sangiovese is a dalliance worth pursuing.

THE TASTING

THE BOTTLE: *Castello di Volpaia Chianti Classico 2018. Tuscany, Italy. $22.*

This Chianti sells itself on looks alone. It's not ruby, it's not laced with purple. It's a perfect shade of Tuscan garnet red. It markets itself as a true wine of Tuscany at first sight.

The smell is unexpected: raspberries, strawberry fruit snacks, and oregano. From my understanding, Sangiovese is often touted as a savory wine, but based on smell alone, it's less savory than I had expected. But no one just stops at smell; tasting is a must.

It's acidic. It's fruity. It's got a hint of Italian spice. It's candied cherries soaked in lemon juice, dried oregano, and hints of oak that leave a slightly buttery aftertaste. Its acidity is surprising to anyone going in for a taste blindly, as I was. But it's a different breed of acid. It doesn't linger on the tongue like other acidic reds. Instead, it stays along the inside of your cheeks much longer than any fruit or spice flavors do. This Chianti is a quick burst of soured cherry candy, sprinkled with dried oregano, finished with a kiss of oak and a smack in the mouth. In all honesty, it seems like the quintessential Italian way of engaging with someone. A kiss and a smack. And I now see why every Italian dinner table needs it. Perfecto.

IN THE WILD

Naturally, Sangiovese belongs on the table if you ever find yourself on the cobblestone streets of Italy. But seeing as how most of us non-Italians are rarely there, a bottle of Chianti is the perfect accent to come forth in a more casual situation: a Friday night in.

The week has been long. Friday took way too long to arrive, and despite your friends' best efforts, you're just not up for a night on the town. You throw on your favorite pair of grey sweats. You order a no-frills pizza, most likely of the Margherita variety. Even though you're staying in, it's still Friday, and that deserves more than Domino's. You queue up a movie you've seen dozens of times already, or perhaps your week has been so draining that the only thing that can help you commiserate properly is anything by Woody Allen, captain of problematic neuroses.

Your pizza arrives, miraculously still hot. You pour yourself a glass of Chianti, and find it to be perfect. It's not trying to fight your pizza, nor does it get lost in the flavors. It's not overly fruity, but it's not overwhelmingly savory. It's the perfect Italian dining accoutrement. And it's just casual enough that it'll happily stick around to soothe your woes until the final credits roll. Or until the bottle is gone. Whichever happens first. It is Friday night, after all.

SYRAH

To find a French bottle, look in: the northern Rhône (Côte-Rôtie, St.-Joseph, Hermitage, Crozes-Hermitage, Cornas)

SYRAH AND SHIRAZ: WHAT'S THE difference? Or, wait, are they the same? In truth, they're just two names for the same grape. But as a wine novice, I didn't even know that Syrah and Shiraz were connected, let alone the same grape. It's not like they put that information on their labels: "Hi, I'm a Shiraz, but technically I'm a Syrah. I just call myself a Shiraz in Australia, because I'm the Jekyll and Hyde of wine grapes." That would be too easy and helpful. Nonetheless, the two types of wine produced from this grape are very different. Syrah is typically produced in France, and Shiraz lives in Australia.

Okay, but why does that matter? Well, flavor for one. And, honestly, that's all that matters in my book. "What can I expect from this bottle?" is all anyone wants to know when contemplating a particular wine, and the Syrah/Shiraz distinction is no exception.

Australian Shiraz is much fruitier tasting because of the warmer climate—the heat means the grapes are much riper at the time of picking. I don't know about you, but I'll take a juicy ripe fruit over an under-ripe one any day. There's also a somewhat smoky kind of spiciness (think tobacco) to a Shiraz, and from time to time, a bold, savory edge.

French Syrah has a more refined style. It houses more subdued fruit flavor, earthy flavors (think moss and fresh-picked herbs), and a more peppery spice. Either way you go, Shiraz or Syrah, you're in for a powerful punch in the mouth, because the Syrah grape carries not a single shy bone in its body.

THE TASTING

THE BOTTLE: *Guigal Crozes-Hermitage 2015. Rhône Valley, France. $24.*

Once again, it's time to dive in to the French pool of reds. Looking at the label, you wouldn't know that this is a Syrah. As I've learned, French wines don't ever list the grape, they only list the region. But, as noted above, Crozes-Hermitage is a notable region for Syrah. So let's see what that pocket of France has to offer.

Turns out, Crozes-Hermitage Syrah smells like plum, mossy forest floor, and peppercorns. Very on par for the French style. There's no sweetened fruit, no candied elements— nothing sweet about it. Then again, if I were raised in stony granite along the Rhône river, I probably wouldn't be categorized as 'sweet' either.

The taste reinforces the smell because, again, the French don't do surprises. There's black pepper, under-ripe plum, and subtle hints of smoked meat and black licorice. Being a powerful grape, it has a tendency to linger in your mouth long after you've finished your sip. The Syrah has a way of making you want to stretch your mouth out if you take too big of a sip, that's how overpowering it is. A vacuum of peppery spice and cheek-drying tannin.

This bottle fits the bill when looking for a classic French Syrah. It's refined, it's spicy, and very serious. As it should be.

IN THE WILD

French Syrah belongs at the right hand of a novelist who writes literary fiction. I imagine novelists of that nature want to be challenged, yet comforted. Inspired, yet refined. Writing about life is serious, contemplative, and more often than not, altogether bittersweet. As it stands, writing literary fiction necessitates a wine that can match.

Syrah is that wine. It's sophisticated and powerful. It's challenging because it requires your attention. It's spicy. It's bitter. It's refined in fruit. It's the perfect wine to complement the plight of a novelist. Who knows? Maybe if Hemingway had a good Syrah, he wouldn't have infamously regretted not drinking more wine.

TEMPRANILLO

SPANISH WINES ALWAYS SEEM TO be in a class all their own. Often forgotten in lieu of more notable "Old World" producers like France and Italy, Spain consistently churns out some of the most renowned wine grapes in the world. Grenache is in everything from its namesake Garnacha, to Rosé, to GSM blends. Cava is Champagne's younger, high-quality sparkling sister finally getting the recognition she deserves. And Tempranillo is no different.

In fact, Tempranillo is so popular that it's considered one of the red noble grapes (amongst the likes of Pinot Noir, Merlot, and Cabernet). When it's young and lively, it's full of juicy, ripe red fruit while maintaining a slightly savory profile. As it ages, it exhibits tobacco and leather flavors. It's quite the developing grape—appreciable at any stage one prefers. It's just as likely to be enjoyed within a year of production as it is 10 years down the line. With so much variety in flavor, you're bound to land on a bottle worth savoring. And a bottle from Rioja is a desirable place to start.

THE TASTING

THE BOTTLE: *Cune Crianza 2016. Rioja, Spain. $13.*

As tempting as it is to buy a bottle of the highly visible Campo Viejo anytime you want a little Spanish flair, for two dollars more, why not find out for yourself how dynamic, yet delicious Tempranillo can be? Cue the Cune.

The "Crianza" designation on a bottle from Rioja signifies that the wine has been aged for one year in oak. "Reserva" bottles are aged longer, and the eldest "Gran Reserva" bottles have been aged more than five years. The more oak-aging, the more vanilla, caramel, butter, baking spice, smoke, cedar, or toasty flavors you can expect from a wine. So, it should be no surprise that this bottle smells of blueberry sauce, strawberry jam, caramel (evidence of oak!), and, if you swirl long enough, a hint of orange peel.

The taste is just as complex. There's cherry, sun-dried tomato, vanilla, a touch of smoke, and, again, the orange peel towards the end. Bursting with flavor, it's red-fruit-jammy, with a toasty savoriness, and it has a smooth, caramelized vanilla edge thanks to its time spent in oak.

Tempranillos from Rioja are easy to drink, yet not considered a 'light' red thanks to their massive flavors, acidity, and, if you can believe it, tannin. On your palate, the tannins are barely noticeable, which makes this wine all the more impressive. With all the in-your-face fruit, lovely savory touches with the sundried tomato, smooth caramelized sweetness, and surprising orange peel, this wine wins you over with every flavorful sip. I'm telling you—Rioja is in a league of its own.

IN THE WILD

Tempranillo from Rioja is the fun, nonchalant, well-traveled aunt who always seems to be jetting off to somewhere new. She always returns from her travels with more wisdom to impart, but insists on keeping every conversation fluid and casual. She's effortless, yet bursting with character and intrigue, approachable yet equally stunning. She's always dazzling everyone she meets, but remains the most authentic person you know.

This Spanish variety is fruity and fun, smooth in an elegantly refined way, and just mysterious enough from the unexpected savory and smoky notes to keep you intrigued. It's nonplussed, classy, and most of all, ready to help toast to a life well lived. Anything less would be a tragedy. ¡Salud! to that.

ZINFANDEL

FOR WHATEVER REASON, ZINFANDEL IS not a wine I've ever taken seriously. Just hearing the name makes me immediately think of cheap boxed wine, jugs of Boone's Farm, or clichéd suburban moms who have no idea what wine actually tastes like. I know, I know, I'm very judgmental and for no good reason, but first impressions matter! And the first time I saw Zinfandel in the wild, it was on the side of a giant box of Franzia being chugged by college students. What was I supposed to think? Delectable, sophisticated grape? I think not. Besides, the United States grows 99% of the world's Zinfandel which, to me, is a red wine flag. Any wine we make exclusively is rarely lauded. Are you familiar with the Concord grape? Of course you are… as the grape of *Welch's grape juice*. Not as a highly esteemed wine grape. So, yeah, I'm a little apprehensive when it comes to Zinfandel.

But, ten years later, I've been forced to be open-minded. That's what this tasting journey is all about. I have to give Zin a second chance and try the jammy hat on once again in an environment where no one needs to "slap the bag" to get a taste. I'm sure spending over $5 will boost my odds tremendously in the flavor department, too. And, in the spirit of not being *too* buttoned up, I rededicated my efforts with a bottle lovingly called "Plungerhead."

THE TASTING

THE BOTTLE: *Plungerhead Lodi Old Vine Zinfandel 2017. Lodi, CA. $13.*

I love this bottle name. It truly reinforces the casual vibe of the Zinfandel grape. Although, to be fair, any Zinfandel sold at over $5 a bottle is worthy of a second chance on looks alone. It's a deep ruby color, not too watery, not too heavy. It's a solid medium-bodied red wine with notes of cherries, raspberries, and holiday spices. Mostly clove. Smells nothing like a box of Franzia, I'll give it that.

Luckily, it tastes much, much better, too. It's like a jar of smoked raspberry jam with spicy gingerbread syrup laced throughout. And the spicy gingerbread flavor lasts well beyond finishing your sip, making your mouth feel like a holiday cookie graveyard. I imagine if you drink enough of it, you'll end up looking like the guy on the bottle with a plunger on his head. Then again, maybe that's exactly what they were going for. Either way, it's much more elevated than any boxed or bulk wine. That smoky jam with holiday spice is well worth the extra $8 in my book.

This is a perfect example of why giving wines a second chance, at a more respectable price point, can pay off. Zinfandel, you're back in my good graces. Thank you for putting up with my scoffing for so long. I'll make it up you, I promise. Especially come holiday season.

IN THE WILD

No doubt, Zinfandel is the wine to drink during the holidays. Actually, let's take it a step further: it's the wine to drink *way too much* of during the holidays. Hear me out. I know Zinfandel is not the first to come to mind when the snowflakes fall. But let me set the all too familiar stage, and you'll see what I'm talking about.

You're at your family's house. Whether it's with your parents, your grandparents, aunts and uncles, or even your in-laws, it doesn't matter. What does matter is that the small talk has expired, dinner won't be ready for another hour, and no one has opened the wine yet. You can't be the first one to reach for it, lest you be labeled someone with a drinking problem. But no one else seems even remotely interested in drinking yet. They're all blithely unaware of the fact that this social situation, forced at a minimum of once a year, is unnatural. Being pummeled with far-too-personal questions, especially coming from people you only see once a year, would make anyone reach for a bottle. You've already run out of passive-aggressive smiles, nods, and curt answers to their interrogations. And you've finally reached the point of caring so little that you don't care if you get side-eyed. It's time for a bottle of Zinfandel.

Now, normally someone brings a Cabernet or Merlot to these occasions of forced merriment, but honestly, both are a bit too uptight for holiday dinners. These holiday gatherings are always awkward, anyway. Heaven forbid you bring along a wine that won't save you in the flavor department, either. Which is precisely why you brought the Zinfandel.

It's fruity and inviting, and the holiday spiciness makes you feel like you just drank a hug. It's a drunken wink and a blown kiss from across the room. Or at least that's what you'll be doing after a few glasses—a far cry from your internal cringing two hours ago. You'll probably even get bonus points if your family likes Pinot Noir or Shiraz. The fruitiness is on par with Pinot, and the spiciness is a friendly nod to an Australian Shiraz. The family will love it so much they'll forget to ask you when you're having kids/getting married/getting a promotion. For once, your requisite holiday get-together is a lot more manageable now that there's a bottle of Zin at the table. Or *was*.

Shall I open another bottle?

NOTES FROM THE OTHER SIDE

(of 25 bottles)

WE MADE IT—MORE THAN two cases of wines later. Of course, this wasn't an endeavor to see how much wine I could drink in a relatively short amount of time. I'm not a collegiate. Nor was this saga meant to teach you everything there is to know about wine. I'm not even qualified for that daunting task. No, this was an adventure. And any worthwhile adventure brings forth lessons, insight, shortcuts, and inspiration. Looking back…

RED WINES ARE NOT AS HOMOGENOUS AS I THOUGHT.

Pinot Noir is as different to Syrah as milk chocolate is to 90% cacao: similar on the surface, but that's where it ends. But you can't truly understand until you sit down with each one and taste for yourself. Thinking all red wines are the same held me back for years, and now that I've sampled 16 of them, I know that not to be true. If anything, I've been convinced that anyone with any palate can find a red wine that suits them, just as they can a white wine.

IT'S OKAY TO NOT LIKE FRENCH WINES.

Wine snobs don't give people a lot of room to have different palates from their own. According to them, not liking French wines is a sin, just as much as enjoying a $10 bottle of oaky Chardonnay from California. But guess what? I don't like a lot of French red wines, and I love Kendall-Jackson Chardonnay. Who cares? Wine isn't about appealing to one person's self-aggrandized taste; it's about finding your own. Forcing yourself to drink varieties you don't like because a critic says so will just make you hate wine in general.

SPARKLING WINES ARE NOT ALL THE SAME. EVEN CHAMPAGNES TASTE DIFFERENT FROM ONE PRODUCER TO THE NEXT.

This was one of the more surprising revelations I had along the way. Call it naivete, call it ignorance. But before my tasting journey, a sparkling wine was a sparkling wine. Whether it came from Spain as Cava, Italy as Prosecco, or France as Champagne, it all tasted the same—until I approached tasting with intentionality. I now know Cava is delicious with added sweetness. Prosecco is the true match for brunch. And Champagne... well, Champagne is a tale of two celebrations.

YOU CAN LEARN TO TASTE BY JUST PAYING ATTENTION.

I always wondered how sommeliers or wine experts could pick out flavors in wine. Were they gifted with elevated tasting abilities? Were their noses finely-tuned by genetics? Nope. They just paid attention where so many of us don't: in the art of flavor discernment.

When we eat and drink, all we need to know is "good, bad, or poisoned." I like it; I hate it; there's something wrong. It doesn't really benefit us to identify cumin in taco meat, unless we're a chef that needs to know those things. So, it's no wonder we can't pick out allspice in a glass of Pinot Noir. We don't pick out individual flavors from anything else we're eating or drinking. But that can change if you want it to. I wanted to. So, I started paying attention.

I looked up tasting notes for wines that were trickier for me to understand (usually reds) and asked myself: do I taste _____? If I had no idea what a flavor tasted like, I'd either get my hands on it and sample or see if Google could explain it to me until I could taste for myself. That's how I learned what allspice tastes like. That's how I learned what red plums taste like. Over time, my ability to pick out flavors got better, all because I tried more, I tasted more, and I paid more attention.

MOST OF THE INFORMATION ABOUT WINE IS IRRELEVANT TO LEARNING ABOUT WINE.

Not once did knowing whether a wine was aged in French oak or American oak affect if I liked it or not. Not once did knowing which hill the vineyard was planted on make a wine taste better in my eyes. Most of the information I found about the wines I tried was inconsequential—no offense to the oenophiles who find it all fascinating.

The only information that was of any use was the wine itself. If I liked the taste of the glass in front of me, I remembered the grape and the region and saved it into my reference sheet of wines I liked. Now, when I'm picking out another wine, I can draw on my tasting experiences and remember that, yeah, I like Chardonnays and Pinot Noirs from California, but not Cabernets. Or, no, Sauvignon Blancs from the United States or France gross me out, but New Zealand is okay sometimes. All the peripheral information out there doesn't do much to help the average Joe/Jolene pick out a wine they'll like. All that really helps is tasting a bunch of wine from a bunch of unique areas and remembering "likes" and "don't likes."

WINE THAT SMELLS OR TASTES LIKE NAIL POLISH REMOVER IS A WINE THAT'S GONE BAD.

Consider this more of a cautionary tale. I was with a friend trying a bottle of Grenache another friend had given him. It smelled horrific—like a nail salon. We texted the friend who gave it to us and he said (along with a face-palm emoji) that it was just a high alcohol wine. But we knew—that was not alcohol we were smelling. That was the smell of nail polish remover—a telltale sign that our wine had gone bad.

Thankfully, we didn't get sick from drinking spoiled wine, because we knew a red flag when we smelled one. In conclusion, never drink a wine that smells or tastes like non-acetone nail polish remover. As if you'd want to anyway.

IF YOU HAVE A BOTTLE OF ROOM TEMPERATURE WINE THAT NEEDS TO BE CHILLED, WRAP IT WITH A COLD, DAMP PAPER TOWEL AND PUT IT IN THE FREEZER FOR 15 MINUTES.

Just don't forget about it for longer than 15 minutes, or else your wine might explode. Otherwise, it works like a charm in a pinch. If you have a room temperature bottle of sparkling wine, put it wrapped in the refrigerator, not the freezer, which will kill the bubbles.

* * *

This tasting journey through 25 wines has taught me a tremendous amount. More than any other book I've come across. It confirmed some of my preconceptions (Sauvignon Blanc is still not my taste), while it shattered others (sorry for hating on you, Zinfandel). I've learned that some wines have distinct personalities on their own (Tempranillo), while others perfectly complement life's ups and downs (Merlot). No matter what, though, wine can and always will have a place in our lives, as an accent or the pièce de résistance, as a destination or a traveling partner. It's there to suit your tastes, your moods, your company, your life. It will always have a purpose for the one who enjoys it. Dare I say, the romance many have with wine is now much easier to see. It just took 25 wines for me to realize it.

I've learned a lot along the way, that's for sure. And yet there's still so much more to discover. There are hundreds more wines out there waiting to be tasted, savored, included. And it would be a shame if I stopped my tasting journey now. So, I won't. I'll continue to seek new grapes, new regions, new vineyards in the hopes of a broader palate and novel tasting experiences. That's the thing about wine, I guess—once you start, once you pay attention, it's hard to stop. You have to keep tasting, keep sampling, keep enjoying this thing that's been around for centuries, marking the lives of Apostles, poets, presidents, and philosophers. And now us.

Join me. Embark on a tasting journey of your own. Sample as much as you can, whenever you can, however you can. And don't forget to bring people with you. The wine would want nothing more than to be surrounded by people who enjoy it— no formal education required. The wine will provide all the education you need. You need only pay attention.

Cheers!

ACKNOWLEDGEMENTS

I couldn't have done it without you.

WRITING A BOOK IS TRULY a labor of love. It's a frustrating, tedious, rewarding leap of faith that wouldn't have been possible without the help of some very important people.

To my parents, Jay and Jill, who despite not being wine drinkers, encouraged me every step of the way to make this book become a reality. I can't thank you enough for your support, understanding, and involvement, even when you (and I) had no idea what I was doing.

To my amazing editor, Nicky Guerreiro, who believed in my idea from the jump. Your insight and dedication to detail (what you call "the copyeditor's curse") was exactly what this book needed. I'm so grateful that you took my little wine book under your wing. This book is better because of you.

To my dear friend Jeremy Dinkins, I would've given up on this ridiculous idea months ago if it weren't for your encouragement. Thank you for always lending a listening ear, trying new wines with me, shooting my author photo, and being an amazing support despite all my anxieties and panics along the way.

Jackie Schmidt, my ride or die, you have always been so supportive of me and this book was no different. Thank you for being my favorite "what if" instigator and believing in me when I was struggling to myself. Even though I always hedged your wild optimism, the fact that you always offered it means the world.

To Kim Jenson, my forever cheerleader and fellow oenophile, thank you for your eternal (now long-distance) support. You've always helped me in any and all capacities, and I'm so grateful to still be a part of your and Tom's life.

Drinking wine is never meant to be a solo sport. So thank you to my all-time favorite wine drinking partners: Ashley Leffler and Kierstin Moddelmog. Ashley, you were my very first partner in crime, and I know wine nights in college were always the best when you were around. I can't wait to open a bottle with you soon. Kier, I wouldn't love Prosecco like I do today if it weren't for our many "spur of the moment" pow-wows over bubbly. You make drinking wine fun, like it should be.

Finally, I wouldn't have been able to drink all of these wonderfully popular wines if I couldn't find quality affordable bottles. So thank you to the Binny's store in Geneva and Algonquin, Illinois. Your massive inventory, wallet-friendly prices, and helpful staff made this whole tasting journey a breeze. And I can't thank your staff enough for not judging a woman buying multiple wines every week for months. I know it probably looked suspect, but this book is proof that I bought those wines with honorable intentions.

Thank you, all of you, for your roles in the creation of this book. You all helped in unique and equally important ways and, because of you, more people will be less confused and frustrated when faced with the daunting task of choosing a wine. Cheers, everyone—we did it!

A SIMPLE FAVOR

Starring: Blake Lively, Anna Kendrick, and Your Honest Opinion

LET ME START BY THANKING you tremendously for taking the time to read *From Cabernet to Zinfandel*. I hope you laughed, learned, and had a blast in a glass learning about the world's most popular wines. If you've gotten this far, you'll know that I have every intention of continuing this journey. Naturally, I'd love to continue sharing this wild wine-fueled saga with you, so that means book number two! More wines, more personalities, more ways to fit the wines of the world into your fabulous life.

But before we dive into 25 more wines, I have a simple favor to ask. If you'd be so kind, I'd love it if you would post a review of *From Cabernet to Zinfandel*. Whether you loved it, hated it, or landed somewhere in between, I'd love to hear your feedback. Reviews are hard to come by for a new author and you, the reader, have the power to make or break a book. It doesn't have to be lengthy, or even a full sentence, just an honest opinion from you would mean the world.

If you can spare the time, head right over to my book's page on Amazon and drop a quick review. You'll be my new hero (even if you hated every last page of it).

Thank you again for spending time with me and my first labor of love, darling reader. I'll see you again for book number two.

In good wines and bad,
Shea

COMING FEBRUARY 2021

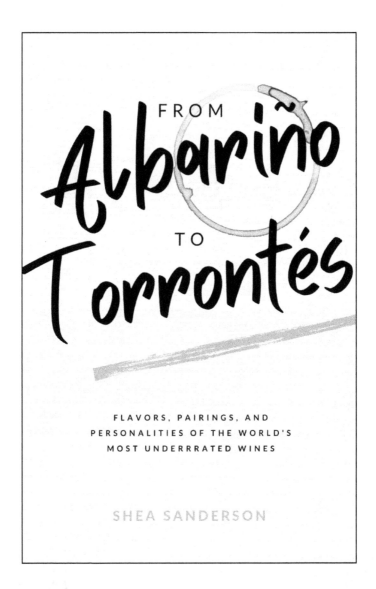

FROM

Albariño

TO

Torrontés

FLAVORS, PAIRINGS, AND
PERSONALITIES OF THE WORLD'S
MOST UNDERRRATED WINES

SHEA SANDERSON